THE ALAMO

THE ALAMO

A Cultural History

Frank Thompson

Taylor Trade Publishing
Dallas, Texas

Frontispiece: Jules Guerin's romantic view of the Alamo by moonlight appeared in *The Ladies' Home Journal*, April 1921. [Craig R. Covner Collection]

For Dallas Leon Nelson—my other brother

Designed by David Timmons

Published by Taylor Publishing Company
1550 West Mockingbird Lane
Dallas, Texas 75235

Library of Congress Cataloging-in-Publication Data
Thompson, Frank T., 1952–
    The Alamo : a cultural history / Frank Thompson.
        p.   cm.
    Includes bibliographical references (p.) and index.
    ISBN 0-87833-254-5 (cloth)
    1. Alamo (San Antonio, Tex.)—Siege, 1836. 2. Alamo (San Antonio, Tex.)—
History. 3. Alamo (San Antonio, Tex.)—Siege, 1836—Influence. 4. Alamo
I. Title.

F390 .T45 2001
976.4'03—dc21   00-066644

10 9 8 7 6 5 4 3 2 1

Printed in the United States of America

Contents

THE ALAMO

Introduction

"What's your name?"
    "I can't remember."
"Where are you from?"
    "I can't remember."
"What do you remember?"
    "I remember . . . the Alamo."

                    Pee-wee Herman
                    Pee-wee's Big Adventure

Just a few weeks before completing this book I was showing my family, visiting from South Carolina, around Los Angeles. My nephew Michael is a high school football coach and obsessed with all things athletic. He was particularly keen on visiting Dodger Stadium and, even though there wasn't a game that day, we went there. We were able to walk around the arena, taking snapshots and soaking in the atmosphere—which, from my point of view, suffers greatly when there are no Dodger Dogs around. We finished our visit by browsing through the gift shop. Now, all who know me will tell you that I am no sports fan. In fact, I seem to be missing the sports gene altogether, much to my family's dismay. Nevertheless, I walked out of the gift shop with a new baseball cap on my head. On the front of the cap were sewn the letters "S.A " for San Antonio, and a picture of the Alamo. My wife Claire took one look and smirked. She said, "Leave it to you to walk into a sports shop in California and find something with the Alamo on it."

My mother didn't seem surprised. She shrugged and said, "The Alamo is everywhere."

Sometimes it seems that this is true. The Alamo stands in the heart of San Antonio, both literally and figuratively. Texans, and people from everywhere else, approach the place with a kind of awe. The Alamo is called the Shrine of Texas Liberty and is treated as such; upon entering the serene building, many feel the same sense of reverence experienced at Lourdes or the Sistine Chapel. The ancient structure is an eternal, melancholy symbol of everything the Texas heart holds dear: sacrifice, heroism, fearlessness. It is a window to the past, and a finger pointing to the future.

But San Antonio isn't the only place that remembers the Alamo. The old limestone church—with its serene face of columns and icon niches that frame a large wooden door, topped by the familiar rounded gable ("the hump")—is one of the most instantly recognized images in the world. It appears in history books, travel guides, and encyclopedias, of course; but it is also routinely reproduced in advertisements, on billboards, on toys, in comic books, and on television. Any tourist who visits San Antonio feels obligated to go there, and have photos snapped while standing in front of it, even if they're a little unsure as to why.

Similarly, virtually every motion picture produced in San Antonio, no matter what the plot or time period, is also compelled to include the Alamo, even when it has little to do with the story. As *Selena* (1997), Jennifer Lopez gives a concert in Alamo Plaza, with the old church looming in the background. Young Henry Thomas becomes involved with spies in the Alamo in *Cloak and Dagger* (1984). Sean Connery thwarts an assassination attempt in front of the Alamo in *Wrong is Right* (1982). Gus McCrae (Robert Duvall) and Woodrow Call (Tommy Lee Jones) saunter past the Alamo, while wondering if they themselves will be remembered, in *Lonesome Dove* (1989). The South Park folks briefly visit the Alamo in *South Park: Bigger, Longer and Uncut* (1999). A beautiful sunrise shot of the Alamo appears under the credits of the romantic comedy *Still Breathing* (1998). And, perhaps most memorably, Pee-wee Herman, desperately searching for his stolen bicycle, finds to his dismay that the Alamo has no basement in *Pee-wee's Big Adventure* (1985).

A webcam broadcasts live pictures of the Alamo on the Internet twenty-four hours a day, and the huge sports arena in San Antonio is

Pretty girls,
pretty girls
everywhere,
But the
SAN ANTONIO
BELLES
are claimed
most fair·

San Antonio, Tex. The Alamo — Built 1718.

To lure tourists to San Antonio, this 1910 postcard offered two kinds of lovely sights. From the author's collection.

called the Alamodome. San Antonio's nickname is, in fact, "The Alamo City." Images of the old mission's remains are everywhere—on police patches; at bus stops; on tee shirts and coffee mugs; on posters, pennants, and postcards.

All of which, of course, is only marginally related to the reason that the Alamo was supposed to be remembered in the first place. Certainly, there are plenty of references around San Antonio to the *battle* of the Alamo, but the building itself seems only barely connected to that bloody event. In the almost 170 years since the Alamo defenders, in John Wayne's words, "lost the battle that won the war for Texas independence," the ancient limestone building has slowly become something else, an icon with a meaning and resonance all its own.

But precisely what that meaning is remains up for grabs, as Alamo authority Paul Andrew Hutton wrote:

> There have always been two Alamos—the Alamo of historical
> fact and the Alamo of our collective imagination. One was a mis-

A snapshot from 1915. From the earliest days of photography, tourists have wanted their pictures taken at the Alamo. From the author's collection.

sion and a fortress, and is now a shrine. The other has become a cultural and political symbol. But symbols have many uses and can be portrayed in many ways. Thus a name enshrined in historical memory has also been used to sell dog food and rental cars, banking services and real estate, history and propaganda.[1]

A perusal of the San Antonio phone book reveals scores of businesses with "Alamo" somewhere in the name. Plumbers, acupuncturists, massage therapists, caterers, insurance firms, undertakers, bail bondsmen, architects, karate instructors, and gardeners—even cheerleaders. They all use the name and, in many cases, the image of the Alamo on their signs, advertisements, and business cards. Businesses—not only in San Antonio, but all over Texas—are even housed in replicas of the Alamo, some impressively realistic, others cartoonishly absurd. (See Chapter Nine for a more thorough discussion of these Alamo replicas.) Questioned about the history of the Alamo, or its meaning in history, how many of those businesspeople would display any but the most rudimentary knowledge of the subject? Yet they have chosen the Alamo not,

Satan remembers the Alamo in Ramsey Yelvington's play, *A Cloud of Witnesses*. From the author's collection.

presumably, because of its connection to slaughter, but because the image is so potent a symbol of the city in which they live.

Ramsey Yelvington's evocative and poetic play, *A Cloud of Witnesses* (1954), makes its own point about the difference between Alamo the place and Alamo the historical event. As the play begins, the ghosts of the Alamo defenders (the "cloud of witnesses") are confronted by Satan. They believe that they still have a message of sacrifice, heroism, and patriotism to give to the world, but Satan isn't so sure:

> *Satan*: It seems that today the term [freedom] is become confused. The meaning is now everywhere debated. It is not clear-cut, as in your time. And your deed, your deaths, though generally revered, are . . . oh, something in a niche; something cloudy in a baroque picture frame. *Great*, of course; but so. . . remote. People and times were so *different* then!

Oh, you have done a fair job of keeping your memory alive, with your general pressures. Politicians wouldn't miss speaking there. Why, that interesting addition they made to the front of the Alamo chapel is one of the most readily identified façades in the world!

(pauses, then ironically:)

Though of course it wasn't there in your day.

Don't you see? The place takes precedence over the ideal! The place is hallowed! The place is a thousand times more photographed than the lesson learned!

Yelvington's point is that the modern world is slowly losing touch with the ideals for which the Alamo heroes are supposed to have died, and it is up to his "witnesses" to reaffirm the principles those heroes stood for. The sentiment is certainly a sound one—the world is inarguably even farther from those ideals today than when Yelvington wrote his play in the early fifties—but the separation of idea and deed regarding the Alamo is perhaps not nearly so ominous as Yelvington's Satan suggests. It simply means that the Alamo has come to have more than one meaning. The famous image of the Alamo has indeed been used for trivial purposes, but it remains one of America's most profound symbols. One could, in fact, argue that as the meaning of the Alamo changes and develops from generation to generation, its image becomes *more* profound. Though nearly everyone can easily identify the building itself, the meaning of the place is not so instantly accessible. The Alamo, which started out as a symbol, has gradually become a trademark—but of what?

Tourists visiting the Alamo today are confronted with a site that would barely be recognized by the men who died there on March 6, 1836. Most of the mission compound has been dismantled over the years. Bookstores, tourist shops, and fast-food businesses occupy the area where the west wall once stood. To the north, the place where Alamo commander William Barret Travis was killed is located behind the service counter of the main post office. The palisade, constructed of

This 1960 ad underscores the deeply cherished idea that the men of the Alamo died for fine groceries at bargain prices. From the author's collection.

wood and earth and said to be the spot defended by David Crockett and his "Tennessee Boys," is long since gone, though a boundary line in the pavement marks its general location. The site of the mission's main gate to the south, and the "low barracks" where historians believe that Jim Bowie died, is now a grassy park that extends all the way to the historic Menger Hotel.

The only parts of the original mission/fortress still standing are the church itself and a select few pieces of the long barracks. But even these only barely resemble their appearance during the battle. In 1836, the long barracks was a two-story building, probably the strongest structure in the fort and certainly the place where the deadliest, most savage fighting took place. The building was virtually demolished when the army "remodeled" it in the 1850s. In 1913, to better emphasize the building that was already commonly called "the Alamo," the tattered remains of the top story were removed (see Chapter Four for a more thorough discussion of this event). The long barracks today is almost entirely a reconstructed building, with very, very few traces of the original structure.

In 1836, "the Alamo" referred to a vast mission compound. Today, it essentially refers to one building. And in the imaginations of most visitors, it is in this single structure where the battle took place. It is said that the most common response by tourists, upon seeing the Alamo for the first time, is, "It's so small." Models, dioramas, and other historical and educational exhibits around the grounds are getting better at explaining the discrepancy between the Alamo today and the fort of long ago. But few visitors leave with an understanding that the Alamo fell, in part, because it was too *big*—not too small. The massive mission compound covered nearly three acres. Even if recent revisions in the number of Alamo defenders are true—historians now believe that there may have been as many as 250 men in the fort, as opposed to the legendary 182 or 189—the garrison was still woefully inadequate to the task of defending that great expanse of walls, some 440 yards in all. Dispersed evenly, each man would have to defend about ten feet of wall. But the Alamo defenders weren't dispersed evenly. Stephen L. Hardin writes:

> Prevailing doctrine allotted a six-man crew to each piece of ordnance. Travis began the siege with about 150 men; if he had followed that rule and manned all available cannon, 114 of his men would have been assigned as gunners. Travis, of course, did no such thing. Fewer men could fire a cannon if necessary, just not so quickly. In fact, it is unlikely that more than three gunners manned any piece of Alamo artillery.[2]

There were also wounded men in the hospital, and many others engaged in different duties, all of which left long stretches of undefended wall to become vast and deadly entrances into the fort. The church building, roofless and ruined, contained a cannon ramp with a handful of guns and a few men to fire them. The women and children of the Alamo huddled in one of the rooms, and the fort's powder magazine, such as it was, was located in another. But little of the battle took place inside the building. The cannon crew, which may have included Almeron Dickinson,[3] James Butler Bonham, and Gregoria Esparza (whose family trembled just a few yards away), was probably finished off very quickly by Mexican soldiers firing from the doorway. If, as legend has it, Robert Evans was killed while trying to blow up the powder, he would be among the very few defenders to actually die in the Alamo church.

But it is this building that has always captured the imagination, probably because of its beautiful and haunting face; and this structure alone is now considered "the Alamo." This notion, of course, has been supported by countless artists over the years. Illustrations in encyclopedias, history books, comic books, and fiction of all kinds often depict the Alamo church standing alone, under attack from swarms of Mexicans. In many of these pictures, the Texan defenders are shown firing from the anachronistic upper windows—and sometimes even from the icon niches, which artists sometimes have confused for openings.

Many early articles about the Alamo, even interviews with survivors of the battle, quite often paint a picture of the battle as if it took place in this building alone. Felix Nuñez claimed to be a soldier under Santa Anna during the siege. His highly suspect account of the battle has contributed many questionable notions to Alamo history.[4] In his interview, published in 1889, Nuñez describes the assault on March 6 ("the fourth day of the siege"):

> At this time our cannon had battered down nearly all the walls
> that enclosed the church, consequently all the Americans had
> taken refuge inside the church, and the front door of the main
> entrance fronting to the west was open.[5]

Survivor Enrique Esparza, who claimed to have witnessed the death of his own father in the Alamo, was interviewed by what seems to have been a very careless *San Antonio Daily Express* reporter in 1907, when Esparza was 84. When Esparza describes his family's arrival at the

Alamo, he seems to be talking about the fort in strictly modern-day terms:

> It was twilight when we got into the Alamo and it grew pitch dark soon afterward. All of the doors were closed and barred. The sentinels that had been on duty without were first called inside and then the openings closed. Some sentinels were posted up on the roof, but those were protected by the walls of the Alamo church and the old convent building. We went into the church portion. It was shut up when we arrived. We were admitted through a small window. . . . I distinctly remember that I climbed through the window and over a cannon that was placed inside of the church immediately behind the window . . . the window was opened to permit us to enter and it was closed immediately after we got inside.[6]

Of course, at that time the Alamo church had no windows on the sides—only two on the face. Therefore, if the Esparza family was admitted "through a small window," they must have already been inside the mission compound. And if they were, why would they have to climb through *any* window? There seem to be two possibilities. First, Enrique Esparza may simply have forgotten many of the details of what happened some seventy years earlier—which is quite understandable. Or, perhaps Esparza's memory was better than this interview suggests. It was common practice at the time for reporters to interview their subjects and then paraphrase them in print. In this case, if Esparza had actually described the Alamo as he remembered it, the picture probably made little sense to the reporter, who simply bent the old man's words to fit the Alamo as it stood in 1907. In either case, most contemporary readers of the interview would picture the modern-day Alamo, not the sprawling compound of 1836.

Another article in the *San Antonio Daily Express* from August 23, 1897, describes a visit to the Alamo by a "typical touring party." They peek into "the little cell near the entrance where the sick Crockett [sic] was slaughtered on his cot" and "the spot where Bowie [sic] drew the death line over which the patriots unhesitatingly crossed and thereby became the priests of their own sacrifice." The tourists obviously don't know anything about the Alamo and its heroes, and their tour guide (who seems more than slightly inadequate to the task) knows even less. But "the portly gentleman at the head of the party" nervously attempts a little historical revisionism:

> "Do you know, I have heard it questioned if this dramatic episode [the drawing of the line] really occurred. It is pointed out that . . ."
>
> His daughter interrupts impatiently, "Oh, you mustn't question anything here. It spoils all the romance. Do hush, papa."

Clara Driscoll, the so-called Savior of the Alamo, would have firmly supported that little girl's viewpoint. Driscoll believed that the church, if not the entire fort, was at least the focal point of the battle. And, as evidenced by her story, "The Custodian of the Alamo" (from her book, *In the Shadow of the Alamo*), Driscoll, like that young tourist, believed in romance.

In the story, a pretty young Alamo tour guide tells a rich and handsome young railroad executive the story of the siege and fall of the Alamo: "'This room,' indicating with a graceful gesture the interior, 'is where the last stand of the heroes of the Alamo was made.'" It is also, according to this daughter of Texas, where Travis drew his line of decision. "'He then took his sword and drew a line with it across the dirt floor of the chapel, and called upon those who were willing to die with him for the sake of their country to step across.'" And finally, the tour guide tells about the last battle: "'The Texans desperately contested every inch of ground until by the overwhelming force of numbers they were forced back into the chapel, where the last stand was made.'"[7]

In this vapid little romantic story, by the way, Driscoll does offer us a rather precious example of the difference in visiting the Alamo in 1906 and going there today. The young tycoon is the Alamo's only visitor on that particular day. As he makes small talk with the lovely young daughter, she checks her watch and says, "I am sorry to turn you out, but I close the chapel at twelve, to go home for lunch."[8]

Author Maurice Elfer, not the world's most diligent historical researcher, only added to the confusion. He described the interior of the Alamo this way:

> Entering the Alamo, one sees a large hall running from the front wall to the rear one. Therein occurred the bloodiest fighting, and

it is in the middle of this large room that Travis drew the heroic line. To the left as one enters there is a small room in which Bowie was sick and was nursed during the siege by Madam [sic] Candelaria, a Mexican woman.

On the other side of the building there is only one room, near the entrance. In that room Bowie was killed, and just outside of its threshold Davy Crockett fell. Travis died in the large room, or hall, and between the entrance of the Alamo and the door last described.[9]

After hogwash like this—and so much more in the same vein—it is easy, in one way, to understand why first-time visitors may be slightly disappointed at the sight of the Alamo. They expect to see a fort, with battlements and guns—a place where they can imagine the thunder and horror of battle, where they can visualize the attacking hordes and pretend to be an Alamo defender, swinging an empty rifle like Fess Parker. But the remains of the Alamo don't look like a fort. As author William Zinsser said, in describing his first visit, "I had the feeling I was in a small Romanesque church in Spain or southern France; stone walls, cool interior, pale light."[10]

This building—restored, remodeled, beautified—has virtually no physical connection to its bloody moment. Visitors want a battleground; instead, they find a shrine. The Alamo as it now stands is, in a very real sense, no longer *itself*, but a *monument* to itself.

I remember being slightly confused during my own first visit to the Alamo in 1963. At the age of eleven, I had virtually memorized Walter Lord's *A Time to Stand* (still one of, if not *the*, best general histories of the Alamo) and came to San Antonio bursting with questions, ideas, and enthusiasm. I was not disappointed in the least and certainly did not find the Alamo too "small." Completely entranced by the place, I went around touching the limestone walls lovingly, as if trying to conjure up some traumatic memory embedded in the stone.

Nevertheless, I found it a little hard to reconcile the park-like setting of 1963 with the battle plan described by Lord. I went to the information desk and proceeded to bombard the poor woman sitting there with question after question, until my father came to drag me away—and rescue her. She said to him, "You ought to take this child down to Brackettville to see the set that John Wayne used for his movie. I think he'll get a much better idea of what the Alamo used to look like." My father, for some reason, agreed that this was a good idea. The next day, he drove my family nearly three hours west from San Antonio to Brackettville, Texas, to the ranch of James T. "Happy" Shahan to see the remains of the Wayne set.

At first sight, I was mesmerized. Just as the lady at the information desk had suggested, at Happy Shahan's "Alamo Village," I got a perspective that was impossible to experience at the actual site in San Antonio. I could imagine the vastness, the sense of desolation and ruin. The set had been blasted to pieces during the epic battle scenes that climaxed Wayne's film, and its ruined walls, black with smoke, only made the experience more evocative to me. Here, away from the clutter and clamor of the city, the imagination could run wild. You could pretend that you really had stumbled upon the ruins of the Alamo, forgotten in the wilderness. You really could run around the walls, firing imaginary guns, clutching at phantom wounds. I had always treasured my Marx "Alamo" playset but Alamo Village was like being *in* a playset. It was the ultimate Alamo toy.

I think, in essence, what I wanted and expected from the real Alamo was the experience as described in Dimitri Tiomkin and Paul Francis Webster's song, "The Ballad of the Alamo":

In the southern part of Texas
Near the town of San Antone
Lies a fortress all in ruins
That the weeds have overgrown.

You may look in vain for crosses
But you'll never see a one
But sometime between the setting
And the rising of the sun
You can hear a ghostly bugle
As the men go marching by
You can hear them as they answer
To that roll call in the sky.

Probably, truth be told, that's what *everyone* who visits the Alamo expects to experience. But most people have a hard time finding that peephole through time. In the middle of a huge urban center, filled with traffic noise and the din of thousands of tourists and residents, it's virtually impossible to "hear a ghostly bugle."

The irony is that the Alamo described in that song existed only briefly, in the aftermath of the battle. And John Wayne's film—for which "The Ballad of the Alamo" was written—is largely responsible for our image of the fort as remote, an island in a vast sea of prairie. In fact, the mission San Antonio de Valero was always just on the outskirts of town. Even at the time of the battle, the town was barely half a mile away; and several houses, huts, and other buildings came right up to the walls of the mission compound. It was not a thing apart from San Antonio, but a *part* of San Antonio. The Alamo did indeed lie in ruins for about a decade after the battle, but during that time, San Antonio continued to creep steadily toward it. Local families routinely took stone and lumber from the mission remains to build or repair their own homes. And some of the structures along the Alamo's west wall were inhabited again within months of the battle. By the time the U.S. Army occupied the site in the 1840s—and eventually added a roof and the familiar "hump" to the Alamo church—it was already *in* San Antonio, not merely near it. Hermann Lungkwitz's painting of 1857 (sketched five years earlier) shows a rear view of an Alamo that is surrounded by a thriving neighborhood. Theoretically, visitors of 150 years ago may have had the very same thoughts as visitors of today: "It's so small" and "I expected it to be more remote."

But even so, I have never quite understood how anyone could be disappointed in a visit to the Alamo. There is no aura of thunder, blood, and death; but the beautiful simplicity of its face, the serenity of the grounds, and the cool quiet of the interior make it seem precisely what its caretakers insist that it is—a shrine. A sign on the door admonishes the visitor:

Be silent, friend
Here heroes died
To pave the way
For other men

Inside, men are asked to remove their hats. Except for one day a year, on March 6, no photography—flash or otherwise—is allowed inside the Alamo. Visitors who talk too loudly are asked, politely but firmly, to bring it down to a whisper.

It is difficult to think of another American historical monument—especially on a former battleground—where such reverence is expected, even monitored. Tourists, who may view their visit to the Alamo as only one component of their vacation or business trip, are sometimes puzzled or put out at being told how to conduct themselves—as if they were naughty children being reprimanded by Teacher. But to the Daughters of the Republic of Texas, who take care of the site, and for all those who are truly moved and inspired by the saga of the Alamo, reverence is a natural response to its dignity as a building and to its bloody, inspiring story. And even if that reverence has to be enforced, the men who died in the Alamo deserve it.

Or do they?

The more we learn about the Alamo, the less simple the story becomes. Passed down from generation to generation as a shining example of heroism, patriotism, and self-sacrifice, the legend of the Alamo is at odds—sometimes significant odds—with the historical event, which was inevitably a far more complex, more human event. It has traditionally been seen as a battle in which a vastly outnumbered band of virtuous white men was overwhelmed by a cruel and pitiless gothic, brown-skinned enemy. The Alamo defenders (read: Texans, read: *Americans*) were fighting for their rights just as their ancestors did at Bunker Hill, and the vicious dictator Santa Anna wanted to squash those rights, even if he had to stoop to massacre and torture and other atrocities to do it.

But gradually, the story has evened out. Research has led to more understanding not only of the people involved in the conflict, but of their motives. The defenders of the Alamo were not simply Texans, but citizens of all parts of the United States, and several countries of the world. The only native Texans among the defenders were the Tejanos—Mexicans who opposed Santa Anna's despotic rules and policies. Just as obviously, the Mexican army did not consist of evil, murderous devils but of men, good and bad, doing their highly unpleasant duty for their country.

Nor were the motivations that led to the fight quite so clear-cut as the myth suggests. While some of the Alamo's defenders genuinely saw their defense of the fort as a fight for freedom, and some even saw it as a stepping stone to independence for Texas, others were actually what Santa Anna thought they were: pirates, renegades, roughnecks, and scofflaws. Many of those who came to Texas from the United States became

Mexican citizens only grudgingly and almost immediately began to resent the differences between the way they were governed by Mexico and the way they remembered being governed in the United States. Revisionists have tended to paint all of the Alamo's defenders with these colors. But the truth is always an unruly thing; the assumption that all of the rebels in the Texas Revolution were bad is just as wrongheaded as the unwavering belief in their holy goodness.

"Historians," writes William H. McNeill, "by helping us to define 'us' and 'them,' play a considerable part in focusing love and hate, the two principal cements of collective behavior known to humanity. But myth making for rival groups has become a dangerous game in the atomic age . . ."[11]

The men of the Alamo were, in reality, a cross section of types. There were scoundrels and lowlifes among the garrison, without a doubt, as there are in nearly any congregation. But there were also idealists and fighters, brave, thoughtful men who wanted a better life not only for themselves, but for all people. In short, the men of the Alamo were only human, with all the failings attendant to humanity; but some of them—maybe most of them—were genuinely great and good men.

The Mexican army was also made up of men of all stripes. Though even the most revisionist of historians can rarely find much good to say about Santa Anna, his officers are generally contended to be gentlemen warriors, cultured and brave. They believed, as did the Army of the Republic in the American Civil War, that they were acting to preserve their country. There is not much evidence that any of them wanted to suppress the freedoms of new Texans—many were quite vocal in their opposition to Santa Anna's barbarism—but they were honor-bound to follow their leader and fight for their beloved Mexico.

Nor were the odds quite as daunting as legend would have it. The legend of the Alamo always turns the Mexican army into a multitude. John Wayne's *The Alamo,* for instance, makes frequent reference to "Santa Anna's 7,000 battle-hard troops." In fact, a force of about 1,500 attacked the fort that March morning. And a great many of that number were raw recruits who had never fired a gun before, much less had any battle training. The men in the Alamo were fewer—although in Alamo research, their number keeps growing as the Mexican army's number keeps shrinking—but they had strong walls to stand behind and plenty of cannon to aim at the attacking soldiers. At best, it was never a fair fight—the end was inevitable—though it was not quite the overwhelming massacre that legend claims.

But just because we learn more about the event that in some ways makes it less pristine as a myth, it doesn't mean that the myth has to die—or that the historical reality has to be denied. To recall Paul Andrew Hutton's earlier quote, the Alamo of history and the Alamo of our collective imagination are two very different things. What we take for history can be as fanciful as any work of fiction. And sometimes the fictions about the Alamo offer their own profound truths. The poems, novels, plays, films, and songs about the Alamo are important ways for us to consider, reevaluate, and celebrate what happened there—and to ponder what the Alamo has meant and continues to mean.

In this book I want to examine the Alamo not simply as an event that took place over thirteen days in 1836, but as an ongoing saga that began in 1718 and shows no signs of ending. Over those three centuries, the Alamo has been church and fort, inspiration and joke, a hearth of patriotic virtue and a hotbed of racial conflict. Its famous façade has been linked with presidents and kings, with the famous and the infamous. And it has spawned an entire cottage industry of toys and games, movies and books, cheap souvenirs and priceless works of art.

The entire amazing adventure of the Alamo involves more than simply that bloody moment so long ago. Its incredible cast of characters— from Davy Crockett to Pee-wee Herman—acts out a pageant of history and horror, tomfoolery and profundity, inspiration and silliness that sometimes reveals more about ourselves than about the Alamo.

The myth of the Alamo is in an almost constant state of revision. We now see the battle with different eyes than we did only a few decades ago. We now question everything, argue every interpretation, fight to establish—or discredit—every new detail or idea. But the Alamo itself remains both a part of, and apart from, its bloody past. The Alamo's benign but mesmerizing face has looked upon horror and triumph, and gazes back at us with all the enigmatic, holy power of the Sphinx. It is a shrine and a tomb, a source of ethnic bitterness and a wellspring of patriotic pride. It is an icon of popular culture as well as a continuing inspiration to poets, playwrights, composers, filmmakers, and writers.

Everyone remembers the Alamo. But everyone remembers it in different ways.

Because it is the only original building standing today, many people believe that the Alamo church was where the entire battle was fought. Artists have frequently supported this idea, as these images illustrate.

Left: George E. Richards's illustration from *The History of the American People* (1918). From the author's collection.

Below: C. Richard Schaare's rather comic-book-like frame from *The Life of Davy Crockett in Picture and Story* (1935). From the author's collection.

An unsigned portrait of Crockett from the 1950s. From the author's collection.

A panel from "The American Adventure," a newspaper comic strip (December 11, 1949). From the collection of Craig R. Covner.

The set for John Wayne's *The Alamo* just prior to production in 1959. From the author's collection.

THE FAR SIDE   By GARY LARSON

The story of
the Alamo
inspires reac-
tions that
range from
reverential
to silly.
From
the author's
collection.

Sunday Comic Strip - Ad for *Viva Max* © 1970 Commonwealth United

In 1836, one of the greatest chapters in U.S. history was written by the brave men who defended "The Alamo." Today, almost every American knows and respects the *historical facts* behind this great heroic event. The few that don't, it seems, are in the moving picture business. You'll see just what we mean as . . .

MAD VISITS JOHN WAYDE
ON THE SET OF
"AT THE ALAMO"

ARTIST: MORT DRUCKER   WRITER: LARRY SIEGEL

A page from the 1961 *MAD Magazine* satire of John Wayne's film. This hilarious piece turned out to be one of the most perceptive reviews of the film ever written. Courtesy of William Gaines, *MAD Magazine*.

An Alamo scene from The Wax Museum in Miami, Florida. From the author's collection.

"Davy Crockett at the Alamo," a tableau from the National Historical War Museum in Washington, D.C. From the author's collection.

CHAPTER 1

The Mission

The Alamo, for much of its history, has been a bad-luck place. This is not news to Davy Crockett, Jim Bowie, or Bill Travis, all of whom found terrible fortune there. But even from the beginning, almost a hundred years before Santa Anna attacked the mission fortress, the Alamo was the scene of one misfortune after another. Its very appearance today is the result of a progression of events, many of them disastrous.

The keystone above the Alamo's doors bears the date 1758, but the mission was actually born some forty years earlier. The first Spanish expedition to what would later become San Antonio de Béxar came in 1690. Governor Don Domingo Teran de los Rios wrote in his journal that the area around the Medina River was "the most beautiful in New Spain" and the local Indians, the Payaya, proved friendly and helpful to the Spanish explorers. The priest of the expedition, Father Mazanet, suggested that the site would be perfect for a new mission.

But it was Father Antonio de San Buenaventura y Olivares who worked to make the mission a reality. Fr. Olivares first visited the place in 1709 and soon began lobbying the viceroy of New Spain for permission to found the mission and urging him to send families as settlers to the region. But even though Fr. Olivares went to Spain and to Mexico City in his quest to get his mission started, it was not until 1718 that the governor awarded Fr. Olivares with possession "of the mission site at the Indian village on the banks of the San Antonio River."[1] Fr. Olivares named his new mission San Antonio de Valero in honor of Saint Anthony de Padua and the Spanish viceroy, the Duke of Valero. San Antonio de Valero was officially established on May 1, 1718. Within

Artist Craig R. Covner's meticulous rendering of the Alamo church in the years just after the battle. It probably looked much like this for decades before the battle, as well. The church was never completed, standing roofless and filled with debris for years. Courtesy of Craig R. Covner.

days, a new presidio, San Antonio de Béxar, and a civil settlement, Villa de Béxar, were established nearby.

Fr. Olivares placed Mission San Antonio de Valero on the banks of San Pedro Creek that flowed south of the presidio at San Pedro Springs. But about a year later, he shifted the mission's location to the west side of San Pedro Creek, presumably because the land better lent itself to irrigation.

The first Mission San Antonio de Valero building was a two-story tower structure, made of stone. It housed both a chapel and priests' quarters. The stone building was surrounded by several thatched huts (called jacals), where the Indian residents of the mission lived. It was located on the east bank of the San Antonio River, where Alamo Street and Commerce Street intersect in modern San Antonio.

San Antonio de Valero might have flourished at this spot; but in 1724, a fierce hurricane leveled most of the mission buildings, so Fr. Olivares moved it once again, this time to the present location of the

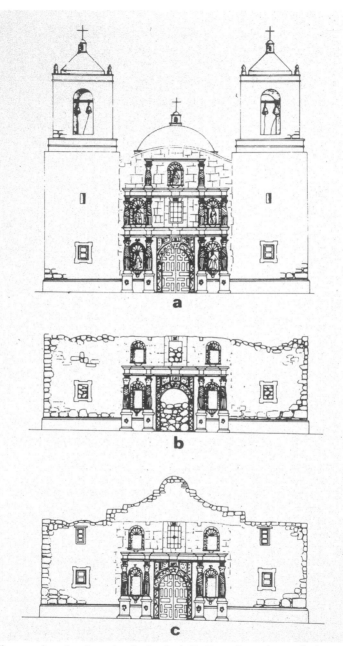

The top drawing is archeologist Jack D. Eaton's conjectural view of how the Alamo church might have been intended to look. At the bottom is the church as it appears today, and in the center is the Alamo as it looked during the battle of 1836.

Mission de la Purisima Concepcion, San Antonio's second mission. From the author's collection.

Alamo. Once there, the mission suffered a series of disasters, including an epidemic that killed almost half of the Indians who lived there. Nevertheless, plans continued to build a permanent mission. Most of the other buildings of the compound were built first, beginning in about 1727, and construction on the new stone church was begun on May 8, 1744. For several years, the little chapel at the former mission site (which had not been destroyed with the rest of the mission) was still equipped to celebrate mass.

Adina de Zavala claimed that the "pretty [new] church with its twin towers, arched roof, and graceful dome was entirely finished about 1757," but there seems to be no clear proof that it was ever really completed. It's something of a moot point anyway, because in about 1757 the church began to cave in, and by 1762 it had completely collapsed—due, says de Zavala, to "the stupidity of the builder."[2] A new church was begun in just about the same spot. Using the same stones from the pile of rubble that was once the *old* church, the operation was supervised by, presumably, a less stupid builder. But although the new architect may have been smarter, he lacked that certain get-up-and-go quality that allows people to actually finish what they start. Despite what we can only assume were his best efforts, the new church was never completed.

Mission San Capistrano. The church, begun in about 1760, was never completed. From the author's collection.

We know approximately how much of the church was built, because we know how much of it was standing during the unpleasantries of 1836. The decoration of the façade had been begun with four icon niches, and carved, spiraled columns framing only the lower two. Two first-floor windows were completed, as were all the ornate carvings around the door. This ornamental entrance had been carved by Dionicio de Jesus Gonzales, who was paid 1,500 pesos for his work.[3] Archeologist Jack D. Eaton created a conjectural view of what the church was apparently supposed to look like. It is a three-level building, with a bell tower on each side. The upper icon niches were also to have been framed by columns, as was a single, centered niche on the third level. The entire structure was to be topped by a dome. The niches were to hold statues of St. Francis and St. Dominic on the first level, St. Claire and St. Margaret of Cortona on the second level, and Our Lady of Immaculate Conception on the third level. The first-level statues were installed and it is possible that the second-level statues were also in place at some point.

Four stone arches, intended to support the dome, were completed.

They were probably demolished in 1835 by General Cos during his fortification of the Alamo. The debris from these arches formed the ramp leading to the apse of the church, where three cannon were placed in the final battle. Adina de Zavala believed that the twin towers and dome had also collapsed into the church; but, though her heart was in the right place, she was often wrong about architectural details.

In about 1758, due to the continuing threat of violence from hostile Indians, the Indian residents and Spanish missionaries constructed protective walls, eight feet high by two feet thick, around the perimeter of the compound. These walls gave San Antonio de Valero an almost fortlike appearance. It was now a position of real strength. Soon enough, it would cease to be a mission and become a full-time fortress.

By the 1770s, the mission life of San Antonio de Valero was apparently in no better shape than the church. The Indians had begun to wander off, relocating their families at the other San Antonio missions. Father John Morfi, after visiting the mission, wrote of its "very decadent condition . . . the residence is uncomfortable and badly kept, showing

Mission San Jose y San Miguel de Aguayo. From the author's collection.

Mission San Francisco de la Espada.

its age and careless construction."[4] Mission San Antonio de Valero was officially secularized in August 1793. It was designated a self-governing pueblo, and its name was changed to Pueblo Valero. Ten years later, a Spanish cavalry consisting of 100 men was sent to occupy the Pueblo. They came from a small town near Parras, Mexico, called San José y Santiago del Alamo. The cavalry unit called itself the Second Company of San Carlos de Alamo de Parras. Locally, they were known as the Alamo Company. And, eventually, the mission-turned-pueblo where they lived was referred to simply as the Alamo.

Over the course of some eighty years, the Mission San Antonio de Valero was devastated by a hurricane, collapsed due to poor workmanship, and had been the site of violence, disease, political intrigue, and warfare. It never thrived as a mission, and only barely qualified as a fort. But as its mission period ended and its military career began, the luck of the Alamo would only get worse. It would eventually become a shining legend and a sacred shrine. But that would be small consolation to those who had suffered there in the past—and to those who, in the winter of 1836, were about to suffer even more.

The Shifting Face of the Alamo

A Visual Essay

The Alamo is one of the most instantly recognizable buildings in the world. Its graceful design of columns, niches and windows—and, of course, its famous "hump"—make the Alamo's façade beautiful yet simple. It is a natural subject for artists, but the image of the Alamo has proven to be remarkably plastic. For a building constructed upon such logical and symmetrical lines, depictions of the Alamo have been, more often than not, fanciful at best. Artists have shown no compunction in changing its shape, dimension, and color. Yet somehow, no matter how bizarrely drawn, the Alamo always reveals itself.

The earliest known depiction of the battle, this 1837 drawing was made by an artist who had no idea what the Alamo looked like—he simply filled in the background with billowing smoke and allowed a kind of castle tower to peek through. From the author's collection.

A year later, in 1838, Mary Ann Adams Maverick made this naïve and fascinating sketch. She was the wife of Samuel Maverick, who was a signer of the Texan Declaration of Independence and, until he left as a courier, an Alamo defender. From the author's collection.

Maverick's sketch was adapted by an unknown artist; this version was used as the frontispiece to Francis Moore Jr.'s *Map and Description of Texas* (1840). This is possibly the first drawing of the Alamo ever published. From the author's collection.

The work of another unknown artist, this drawing was first published in Arthur Ikin's *Texas* (1841). Note that the statues are clearly visible in all four niches of the church, as they are in Mary Maverick's drawing. No one knows when the statues disappeared or what happened to them. From the author's collection.

A true picture of the Alamo church finally emerged in 1849 in this remarkable daguerreotype—the earliest known Alamo photograph, and the only one to show the skyline prior to the addition of the humped gable a year later. Courtesy of the University of Texas, Austin.

RUINS OF THE CHURCH OF EL ALAMO.

This prettified view of the Alamo appeared in *Gleason's Pictorial Drawing Room Companion* in 1854. Probably based on Edward Everett's more accurate drawing of 1850 (see Chapter Three), this Alamo is riddled with niggling errors (the spirals on two of the columns run in the wrong direction) and is too large by half—unless the visitors at the door are leprechauns. From the author's collection.

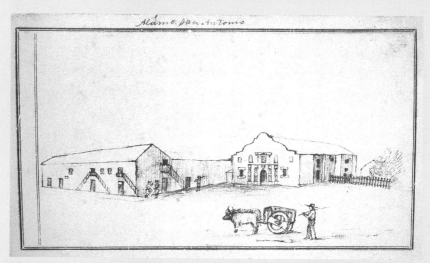

This rare sketch was made by traveler Phocian R. Way in 1858. The Alamo is no longer a ruin but a thriving U.S. army base. The long barracks have been remodeled and built up; and the church now has a roof, several more windows on the front, sides, and back, and its new humped parapet. From the collection of Craig R. Covner.

This drawing from *Harper's Weekly* (March 23, 1861) shows the surrender of U.S. troops to the Confederate Army under General Twigg. The depiction of the Alamo is unusual in several ways: The proportions of the building are off, the spiraled columns have become classical statues, and, in an odd skewing of perspective, the south-wall gate seems to sit *beside* the church rather than several yards to the southeast. From the author's collection.

This exciting battle scene by Armand Welcker features a skyscraper Alamo in close proximity to a San Antonio that looks like a major metropolis. Alamo defenders are grouped not only in the windows of the church but in the icon niches as well. This illustration first appeared in Buffalo Bill Cody's *Story of the Wild West and Camp-Fire Chats* (1888). From the author's collection.

A panel from the comic book *Jim Bowie, the West's Greatest Fighter* (1956). The artist neatly solves the problem of how the battle could have been fought in such a tiny structure as the Alamo by simply expanding the building to full fort size. From the collection of Paul Andrew Hutton.

H. Charles McBarron's Alamo church is a huge, sprawling thing with a face that resembles the Alamo but a size and shape all its own. This painting, "The Alamo," was originally issued in 1963 by American Oil Company as one of a series of prints on American themes. Courtesy of American Oil Company.

Another huge, looming Alamo—clearly modeled on the replica from John Wayne's 1960 film—serves as backdrop to this battle scene in the 1970 comic book *Western Gunfighters*. Here, the Alamo defenders occupy a narrow courtyard in front of the church, with the gate on the north side instead of the south. Oddly, the Alamo appears several times in this story, titled "Call them . . . Renegades," and never looks the same way twice, which is consistent with the artistic history of the Alamo as a whole. From the author's collection.

The Fortress

As the sun set over San Antonio, Texas, on March 6, 1836, a dense haze hung over the city, drifting on the southwest winds from the ruins of an ancient mission on the outskirts of town. This holy place had been baptized in blood earlier on that Sunday morning, as an assault force of the Mexican army under General Antonio Lopez de Santa Anna attacked the besieged defenders of the Alamo and slaughtered every one of them. The day began in fury but ended in a pall of stillness and smoke. But it was not just the smoke of battle that lingered over the Alamo. The conquering Santa Anna had ordered the bodies of the Alamo's defenders gathered into three funeral pyres, soaked with lantern oil, and burned. The thick plumes rising from these pyres darkened the evening sky.

As Santa Anna surveyed the carnage that day, one of his generals said to him, "It was a great victory."

Santa Anna replied with a shrug, "It was but a small affair."

In almost every way, he was right. On that day in 1836, the mission San Antonio de Valero was already nearly a hundred years old and in terrible repair. Despite some hasty fortifications, it could hardly qualify as a real fort. It was manned by somewhere between 188 and 250 defenders, and attacked by a force that probably didn't exceed 1,500 Mexican soldiers. The Alamo was under siege for less than two weeks—during which virtually no blood was shed and no lives were lost—and it all culminated in a surprise predawn attack that lasted well under an hour. In comparison with any of the major battles in history—Waterloo, D-Day, Gettysburg—the siege and fall of the Alamo doesn't seem like much.

Santa Anna. From the author's collection.

But Sam Houston and his avenging army, with their battle cry of "Remember the Alamo!" would soon transform the ruined and bloodied walls of the Alamo into a pristine, mythic celebration of patriotism and inspiration. Houston knew that as an event, the massacre at the battle of the Alamo held little or no military distinction. But as an idea, it could grip the minds of people everywhere, and it could lead to independence for Texas.

Panel from Jack Jackson's *Los Tejanos* (1979). Courtesy of Jack Jackson.

Because the Alamo has such a strange allure to many of those pilgrims who have visited the site over the years, it's tempting to ascribe similar feelings to the men who defended it during those thirteen days in 1836. Such a temptation probably springs from wishful historical thinking of the most banal kind. There is not much evidence that Travis, Bowie, or Crockett ever saw the place as anything more than a second-rate fort, grossly inadequate to the task at hand. But how else can we understand why they decided to make their stand at the Alamo, of all places? In artist-historian Jack Jackson's terrific graphic novel *Los Tejanos,* he pictures Travis and Juan Seguin regarding the Alamo, while Travis's men construct the wooden palisade. Travis says, "There's something magical about the place, don't you think?" But Seguin is simply puzzled. To him, the Alamo is nothing more than the crumbling old mission that has stood on the outskirts of town throughout his life.[1]

Even Walter Lord, when describing one of Travis's letters to Governor Smith, claims, "[Travis] went on to say he would leave in an instant, were it not for the Alamo. But he too had fallen under the spell: 'It is more important to occupy this post than I imagined when I last saw you. It is the key to Texas . . .'"[2]

James Bowie just might have fallen under that same spell. Sam Houston believed the war should be of the "cut, slash, and run" variety, writing in a letter of March 17, 1836, "Our forces must not be shut up in forts where they can neither be supplied with men nor provisions. Long aware of this fact, I directed, on the 16th of January last, that the

*W.B. Travis
By Wiley Martin
Dec. 1835*

Left: William Barret Travis believed that San Antonio and the Alamo were the key to Texas. From the author's collection.

Right: James Bowie may have been sent by Sam Houston to destroy the Alamo. Instead, he decided that he would "rather die in these ditches than give it up to the enemy." From the author's collection.

artillery should be removed, and the Alamo blown up."[3] It was James Bowie who rode into San Antonio with those orders, which Houston clarified in a letter to Governor Smith on January 17, 1836:

"I have ordered the fortifications in the town of Béxar to be destroyed, and if you think well of it, I will remove all the cannon, and other munitions of war to Gonzales and Copano, blow up the Alamo, and abandon the place." But Bowie, once in San Antonio, could never bring himself to destroy the fortress. By February he, like Travis, was convinced of the Alamo's importance, writing, "Colonel Neill and myself have come to the solemn resolution that we will rather die in these ditches than give it up to the enemy."

Left: David Crockett didn't care much for the Alamo. He said he would rather fight out in the open. "I don't like to be hemmed up." From the author's collection.

Below: This oddball view of the Alamo compound features an outsized church with a huge, peculiar hump, and no west wall at all—just a line of shacks. This illustration by Herb Mott is from William Weber Johnson's children's book, *The Birth of Texas* (Boston: Houghton Mifflin, 1960). From the author's collection.

Travis answers Santa Anna's demand for surrender with a cannon shot. Because this is from the *Classics Illustrated* comic, "Davy Crockett," Davy actually gets to do the honors, with Travis's blessing. From the author's collection.

No matter how fanciful our ideas are about Travis and Bowie's spiritual connection to the Alamo, it's pretty clear that "high private" David Crockett didn't care much for the place at all. Alamo survivor Susannah Dickinson, wife of Alamo defender Lieutenant Almeron Dickinson, later recalled that Crockett had said, "I think we had better march out and die in the open air. I don't like to be hemmed up." The truth is, we can never know what was truly in the hearts and minds of the men there, and any feelings we ascribe to them in retrospect are likely to reveal more about ourselves than about them. We have developed a reverence for the Alamo, so we assume that the men who defended it to their deaths shared that reverence. That is almost certainly hogwash. Or, to put it more kindly, that's the myth, not the reality.

It is not within the scope of this book to provide a full, authentic account of the siege and fall of the Alamo (actually, it seems beyond the scope of *any* single book!). But it is worth reviewing the basic story to help the reader unfamiliar with Alamo history to get a general sense of things. More crucially, it gives us a jumping-off point to discuss what has been done with the story over the past 170 years.

The prevailing notion has always been that the battle of the Alamo

MONUMENT ERECTED

TO

THE HEROES OF THE ALAMO,

AND NOW STANDING AT THE ENTRANCE TO THE STATE HOUSE AT AUSTIN, TEXAS,

INSCRIPTION ON THE SHAFT. NORTH FRONT.	INSCRIPTION ON THE WEST FRONT.	INSCRIPTION ON THE SOUTH FRONT.	INSCRIPTION ON THE EAST FRONT.
TO THE GOD OF THE FEARLESS AND FREE IS DEDICATED THIS **ALTAR** MADE FROM THE RUINS OF THE **ALAMO**	BLOOD OF **HEROES** HATH STAINED ME LET THE STONES OF THE **ALAMO** SPEAK THAT THEIR IMMOLATION BE NOT FORGOTTEN.	BE THEY ENROLLED WITH LEONIDAS IN THE HOST OF THE MIGHTY **DEAD.**	Thermopylæ HAD HER MESSENGER OF DEFEAT, BUT THE **ALAMO** HAD NONE.
MARCH 6TH 1836 A. D.	MARCH 6TH 1836 A. D.	MARCH 6TH 1836 A. D.	MARCH 6TH 1836 A. D.

Crockett   Bonham.   Travis.   Bowie.

The first Alamo monument in Austin, Texas. It bore the famous phrase, "Thermopylae had her messenger of defeat, but the Alamo had none." The monument was carved in 1841 using actual stones from the Alamo. In 1881, when fire destroyed the state capitol building, the monument was lost. From the author's collection.

was a battle between "Texans" and "Mexicans"; however, this is not quite true. Yes, a large Mexican army attacked the fort, but most of the Alamo's defenders were Mexican citizens, too. In order to take up residence in Texas, immigrants had to apply for Mexican citizenship and convert to Catholicism. For years, the Mexican government, as part of its plan to attract settlers to help develop this huge area, offered 4,428 acres of land—for free—to any individual or family who wanted to come and live there. Under the Mexican constitution of 1824, the new arrivals wouldn't even have to pay taxes for a full decade. To the thousands of colonists who accepted the offer, this seemed too good to be true.

People came from all over the United States—Tennessee, South Carolina, Georgia, Virginia, Illinois, Massachusetts, Pennsylvania, Louisiana, and many other states—to build new futures in this wonderful new Texas. The call went out beyond the United States, as well. Texas attracted settlers from nearly every country in Europe, including France, Germany, England, Ireland, Scotland, and Denmark.

The vast Texas territory was advertised as a kind of paradise, and, indeed, to those who came to settle there, it seemed like one. The land was rich and fertile, the game was plentiful, the promise unending. Later Texas was called "a heaven for men and dogs and a hell for women and oxen," but in those early days of settlement, its seemingly limitless potential made it seem almost magical. As Walter Lord wrote, "It was enough to give birth to a Texas penchant for superlatives that was destined to endure."[4]

But what didn't endure was the Mexican government's benevolence. By 1830, there were no more Mexican land grants available to outsiders. Worse, Mexico's president and dictator, Antonio Lopez de Santa Anna, decided to ignore the Constitution of 1824 and rule the country his own way. Mexico had always disapproved of slavery, but more and more immigrants, especially those from the American South, were bringing slaves with them into Texas. The practice was officially outlawed in April 1830, outraging those landowners who relied on the abhorrent system to work their farms. Colonists across the board were further angered by another element of the same law, which took away from them the exemption of duty taxes for all imported goods. Even those who had lived in Texas for more than a decade objected to paying taxes—and most of them just didn't bother.

As more and more of their perceived "freedoms" began to disappear, the settlers became ever more resentful. Nearly 75 percent of all new citizens in Texas had come from the United States, and many now began to advocate Texas's independence from Mexico. Others began talking about starting a revolution.

Stephen F. Austin was Texas's leading colonist. He had been chief among the *empresarios* to begin attracting settlers to Texas years earlier. Now, he felt betrayed. Austin urged the colonists—who were by that time calling themselves "Texians"—not to act rashly. In 1833, he decided to go to Mexico City himself to present Santa Anna with a petition, demanding that the dictator restore the Texans' rights to them as guaranteed by the 1824 Constitution. Santa Anna, in true dictatorial fashion, summarily tossed Austin into prison, where he remained for almost two years. Upon returning to Texas in 1835, Austin urged his fellow colonists to prepare for war against Santa Anna.

The first armed conflict came at the settlement of Gonzales in October 1835. A troop of about a hundred Mexican soldiers had been dispatched to retrieve a six-pound cannon that the settlers had been given years earlier. When they arrived, the Mexicans couldn't find the cannon. What they found instead was a defiant group of about eighteen armed colonists who called out that if the soldiers wanted the cannon, they could "Come and take it!" After an uneasy standoff lasting a couple of days, gunfire rang out at about dawn on October 2. The first shot might well have been accidental, but the result was a clear victory for the Texians; the Mexican soldiers broke and ran. The little ruckus killed no one—probably wounded no one—but it was immediately perceived as the Texas version of Lexington and Concord. These shots might not have been heard round the world, but the impact reverberated strongly all the way to Mexico City.

Santa Anna had already sent General Cos into Texas to occupy San Antonio de Béxar, the largest town in Texas and the territory's most important strategic point. Cos was instructed to put down all rebellion by the Texians. When he heard that the revolution had started at Gonzales, Cos moved his troops into the Alamo, just east of Béxar, across the river. Once there, Cos's 1,000 men helped to strengthen the Alamo's walls and otherwise fortify the place; the general was ready to make the upstart Texians surrender.

But it was Cos who surrendered.

About 300 Texians laid siege to Béxar and the Alamo for the better part of a month. Mired in indecision, Texian general Edward Burleson could not quite bring himself to order an attack. A fighter named Ben Milam felt no such hesitation. On December 4, he called out, "Boys, who will come with old Ben Milam into San Antonio?" The men cheered Milam and stepped to his side. Together, they began to prepare their attack.

Before dawn the next day, the Texians began a fight that would continue for four torturous days, systematically moving from house to house. Sadly, one of the few Texians to be killed in the assault was Ben Milam himself, shot by a sniper near the Veramendi Palace. Once the town was in Texian hands, they moved on to the Alamo and took the fort as well. By December 9, Cos admitted defeat. He surrendered, but the Texians allowed him to go free, under the condition that neither he nor his officers would ever again "oppose the re-establishment of the Federal Constitution of 1824." Cos agreed, and led his men south, back to Mexico City.

To Santa Anna, Cos's defeat was embarrassing and infuriating. The handful of Texian colonists should have been taken care of with a minimum of fuss, and here they had sent his general running with his tail between his legs. This time, he swore, he would do the job himself—and do it right. He began marching toward San Antonio at the head of an army of several thousand men, including General Cos.

Meanwhile, the Texians continued the job that Cos started, that of fortifying the Alamo. Under the direction of Green B. Jameson, a former lawyer who had become the Alamo's engineer, the men tried to shore up the crumbling walls and try to make the rambling mission compound into something that could reasonably be considered a fort. Jameson found the task challenging, to put it mildly. In a letter to Sam Houston on January 18, 1836, he wrote, "You can plainly see . . . that the Alamo was never built by a military people for a fortress; though it is strong, there is not a redoubt that will command the whole line of the fort, all is in plain wall and intended to take advantage with a few pieces of artillery." Still, James admitted that it was "a strong place" and well-armed with cannon. In case of attack, he promised, the Alamo defenders could "whip 10 to 1 with artillery."

But no matter how confident Jameson seemed, he realized that the Texians were in a potentially bad position. Only a month earlier, General Cos hadn't been able to hold this sprawling old mission with a thousand soldiers. And the Texians were now proposing to do so with fewer than 300 men.

Actually, by the time Jameson wrote to Houston, there were even fewer than that. Many of the Texians believed that the revolution should be fought farther south, in Matamoros. More than half of the men in the Alamo marched away in early January, taking most of the garrison's ammunition and supplies. That left Commander J. C. Neill in charge of just about 100 men—and those men were dressed in rags and nearly starving.

But help was on the way. Sam Houston sent the famous knife fighter and adventurer Jim Bowie to San Antonio, apparently with orders to blow up the Alamo and other fortifications in town and move the troops out. But once there, Bowie agreed that the Alamo was the perfect place to mount a defense of Texas. He saw its faults as a fort as well as Jameson did, but its many cannon made it seem almost viable as a fortress. He wrote Governor Smith that, far from destroying the Alamo, he and Neill had decided that they would "rather die in these ditches than give them up to the enemy."

On February 3, William Barret Travis arrived at the Alamo with about thirty men, and orders from Governor Smith to take command. Travis was a former lawyer, but now held the rank of lieutenant colonel.[5] Travis was something of a firebrand, given to rather theatrical displays of valor. However, he was indisputably brave and a born leader. He came to the Alamo prepared to give the garrison a backbone of military discipline.

Travis would become famous because of his heroism as the commander of the Alamo, but he was followed into the fort on February 8 by a man who was already famous: former United States Congressman David Crockett from Tennessee. Crockett had a rather outsized reputation as an Indian fighter and bear hunter, and he was known for his tall tales and folksy ways—he was a kind of nineteenth-century Will Rogers. Upon Crockett's arrival in San Antonio, the politician in him came out, and he immediately gave a speech: "I have come to aid you all that I can in your noble cause," he said. "I shall identify myself with your interests, and all the honor that I desire is that of defending as a high private, in common with my fellow citizens, the liberties of our common country." Crockett's presence in the Alamo made for an enormous boost in morale. The men undoubtedly felt that this legend's arrival foretold a victorious future.

On February 24, 1836, Santa Anna arrived in San Antonio de Béxar with his army. He immediately ran up a red flag in the tower of San Fernando Cathedral, about half a mile away. The red flag meant that he would give no quarter. If the men of the Alamo surrendered, they would have to do so on his terms.

Nevertheless, it seems that Travis and Bowie made at least some overtures toward ending the incident before things turned violent. But Santa Anna made it clear that they could surrender only at his discretion. They knew that he had a history of executing prisoners and had no doubt that, in this case, surrender would mean death.

We don't know exactly what kind of flag flew from the walls of the Alamo, but legend has it that the banner was red, white, and green, like the Mexican national flag. But instead of the Mexican eagle, the Alamo flag had the numbers 1824 written on it, to remind Santa Anna of the Constitution that he had abolished. Most historians now discount this idea. Travis bought a flag on his way to Texas and flew it at the Alamo, but no description of it survives. And a company from Louisiana, called the New Orleans Grays, brought their own flag with them; it is the only Alamo flag that survives—barely—in Mexico City. The Grays' flag features the words "First Company of Texas Volunteers from New Orleans." In its center is an eagle with wings outspread, under which is printed, "God & Liberty." Mexican Lieutenant José Maria Torres was killed taking down this flag toward the end of the battle. It was sent back to Mexico City later, but was never displayed publicly. Author Walter Lord reported that when he saw it in the late 1950s, it was "crumbling to pieces in brown wrapping paper."[6] Today, the flag remains locked away, and all efforts to return it to the United States have failed.

When Santa Anna ordered the Alamo garrison to surrender, Travis answered the demand with a cannon shot from the eighteen-pounder in the southwest corner of the fort. The Mexican army then began bombarding the Alamo around the clock, endlessly firing cannon shells into the crumbling fort. Day after day, the shelling continued.

Soon the men in the Alamo were exhausted. Never knowing when the much larger army might attack and overwhelm them, their nerves were shattered. They were losing hope. Travis wrote several letters asking for reinforcements. But the most famous one was written on the second day of the siege. It has become one of the greatest of American documents.

Commandancy of the Alamo,
Béxar, Feb'y. 24th, 1836.

To the People of Texas & All Americans in the world—
Fellow citizens and compatriots—
I am besieged by a thousand or more of the Mexicans under
Santa Anna—I have sustained a continual bombardment & can-
nonade for 24 hours & have not lost a man—the enemy has
demanded a surrender at discretion, otherwise the garrison are to
be put to the sword, if the fort is taken—I have answered the
demand with a cannon shot, and our flag still waves proudly
from the walls—I shall never surrender or retreat. Then, I call on
you in the name of Liberty, of patriotism & everything dear to
the American character to come to our aid with all dispatch—
The enemy is receiving reinforcements daily and will no doubt
increase to three or four thousand in four or five days. If this call
is neglected, I am determined to sustain myself as long as possible & die like a soldier who never forgets what is due to his own
honor and that of his country.

Victory or death.
William Barret Travis
Lt. Col. Comdt.

P. S. The Lord is on our side—when the enemy appeared in sight
we had not three bushels of corn—we have since found in deserted houses 80 or 90 bushels & got into the walls 20 or 30 head
of Beeves.

Travis

According to the traditional histories of the Alamo, Travis's appeals
for help brought only one response. Thirty-two men from the town of
Gonzales arrived at the Alamo on the night of March 1. But new evidence suggests that a second group of reinforcements arrived late on the
night of March 4. If this is true, the number of Alamo defenders might
have risen to about 250. Even so, there were still not enough men to
effectively defend the place. Meanwhile, Santa Anna's army in San
Antonio had grown to at least 5,000 soldiers.

James Butler Bonham was Travis's childhood friend. They knew each other when they were growing up in Saluda, South Carolina. Of all the messengers that Travis sent out from the Alamo, Bonham was the only one to come back to report the results of his mission. His message for Travis and the men of the Alamo has traditionally been presented as a terrible one—there would be no more reinforcements. The dire consequences implied by this message have given Bonham a particularly heroic stature even among this garrison of heroes. By riding back into the Alamo with his message of doom, the legend goes, Bonham knew that he was giving up his life. Yet he had pledged to report the results of his mission to Travis "or die in the attempt." It turns out that he did both.

Then comes the great moment of the Alamo myth. It is said that when Travis received Bonham's news and realized all hope was lost, he called the men together and drew a line in the sand. After outlining the truth of their situation, Travis asked all those who were willing to stay and die in the Alamo to cross the line and step over to him. The only man who chose not to stay was a Frenchman named Louis Rose. Because he was older than most of the men in the fort, he was nicknamed "Moses." Moses Rose, the story goes, jumped over the wall and got away and lived for many years, telling about his escape from the Alamo.

On the night of March 5, the Mexicans' cannon suddenly stopped firing. After almost two weeks of the deafening noise and the nerve-wracking terror inside the Alamo, this silence was like a dream come true. Too tired to be suspicious, many of the defenders fell into a deep sleep. Travis stationed three sentries outside the walls to alert the fort of any attack by the Mexican army. These sentries must have been killed very quietly, for they were never heard from again.

Very early in the morning of March 6, 1836, the exhausted men of the Alamo were awakened by the blaring of bugles, the firing of cannon and muskets, and the sound of thousands of voices crying, "Viva Santa Anna!" The Mexicans were attacking.

Travis leapt from his cot, grabbed a shotgun and sabre, and ran for his post on the north wall. Crockett and his men are believed to have defended the long wooden palisade that connected the Alamo's church to the compound's gate and "low barracks." Jim Bowie had been gravely ill for several days. He was lying on his cot in the low barracks, armed with pistols and his famous knife.

Tapley Holland is the first defender to cross Travis's line in the sand. From the author's collection.

As the shining moment of Alamo myth, the line has been depicted in many Alamo plays, novels, poems, and films.

Travis (Don McGowan) draws the line as Davy and his pals ponder their situation in the Walt Disney television production, "Davy Crockett at the Alamo" (1955). Courtesy of Walt Disney Prod.

Casey Biggs's Travis draws an IMAX-sized line in *Alamo . . . the Price of Freedom* (1988). Courtesy of Rivertheatre Associates

In this conceptual painting by Petko Kadiev for *Viva Max* (1969), modern-day General Max, occupying the Alamo, draws a line with his boot heel, asking every soldier who wants to abandon the post to cross over. Every man promptly does so. From the collection of Craig R. Covner.

The 1953 feature *The Man from the Alamo* was very loosely based on the legend of Moses Rose, the man who *didn't* cross Travis's line. In this film, his name was Stroud, he was played by Glenn Ford (center, hatless), and naturally enough, he turned out to be a hero after all. Courtesy of Universal Studios.

Inside the Alamo's church several women and children huddled, trembling in fear. They were the families of some of the Alamo's defenders. Young Enrique Esparza could see his father Gregorio at his post on a cannon ramp at the back of the church. Susannah and Angelina Dickinson, the wife and baby daughter of Lt. Almeron Dickinson, would never see him alive again.

The Alamo's powder supply was also located in the church. The men had decided that if it looked like the battle was lost, someone should blow up the powder, killing as many of the enemy as possible and keeping the ammunition out of the Mexican army's hands.

During the first wave of the assault, the Alamo's guns cut down many Mexican soldiers. In the darkness and confusion some of the Mexicans were accidentally shot by their own men, and then trampled by running soldiers.

Travis was killed almost at once, and perhaps the first to die; he was hit in the forehead by a single musket ball. The Alamo's commander fell beside his cannon in a sitting position and died as the Mexican soldiers poured past him into the Alamo compound.

The Alamo's biggest cannon, which fired eighteen-pound shells, was in the southwest corner of the fort. As the Mexicans swept over the north wall and toward the church, some Texians turned the cannon around and fired it into the mass of enemy soldiers. The cannon crew was immediately overpowered and killed. Then the Mexicans began using the eighteen-pounder themselves.

Many of the Alamo defenders retreated into rooms of the long barracks, which had been fortified as much as possible. They were determined to fight it out man to man if they had to. But the Mexicans used the Alamo's own cannon against them, firing into the doors of the long barracks, killing or stunning the men inside. The remaining defenders fought savagely, using their empty rifles as clubs, slashing with their great knives, selling their lives as dearly as possible.

Bowie was already very close to death by the time the Mexicans entered his room. He may have defended himself for a while but, in his weakened condition, probably died quickly. It's also possible he was dead before the battle even began.

The men at the palisade found themselves attacked from several sides. They fought fiercely but were terribly outnumbered. Major Robert Evans grabbed a torch and made a run for the powder magazine, hoping to blow it up, but he was shot down before he could reach it. Using Texian cannon, the Mexicans blew down the doors of the church and swarmed over the small cannon crew up on the ramp. Gregorio Esparza fell dead at the feet of his son, Enrique.

Most of the defenders were by that time dead, but it took a while for the firing to die down. A few survivors, hurt and exhausted, were found. A gallant Mexican general, Castrillon, offered to protect them but Santa Anna angrily reminded him of his orders of no quarter. The dictator demanded that the survivors be killed. According to Mexican eyewitnesses, these last members of the Alamo garrison died as bravely as the rest of their comrades.

As the first light of dawn streaked across the Alamo grounds that day, the scene was truly horrible. In and around the fort lay nearly 200 slain defenders and about 600 dead or wounded Mexican soldiers. As Santa Anna looked around, proud of his victory, the women and children of the Alamo were brought before him. Mrs. Dickinson had been wounded in the leg by a gunshot. But she was too stunned by the loss of her husband to notice the pain. Gregorio Esparza's widow and her children asked to be allowed to take his body from the fort to be buried. Santa Anna gave his consent. Esparza was the only Alamo defender to receive a burial. The rest—Crockett, Travis, Bowie, Bonham, and the others—were stacked in funeral pyres and their bodies were burned.

Santa Anna called the battle "a small affair." But the thirteen days that the Mexican army spent laying siege to the Alamo gave General Sam Houston time to raise a real army. About six weeks later, on April 21, 1836, Houston and his angry men attacked Santa Anna's army at a place called San Jacinto, near what is now the city of Houston, Texas.

Houston knew that the men in his ragtag army needed more than bullets to win such a fight. They needed inspiration. So, as his men prepared to attack, Houston called to them, "Remember the Alamo!" They remembered. And as they ran down the sloping ground to overwhelm Santa Anna, nearly every man shouted the Texians' new battle cry, "Remember the Alamo!"

The battle of San Jacinto was over in just fifteen minutes. Santa Anna's army was defeated. The general himself was captured and surrendered his forces to Houston. From that day on, Texas was an independent republic. Nine years later, Texas was admitted into the United States. The Lone Star State has had a glorious history. But that history

From the pop-culture viewpoint, there isn't much doubt about how Davy Crockett died at the Alamo—he went down swinging Ol' Betsy.

Robert Barratt as Davy in *Man of Conquest* (1939). Courtesy of Republic Pictures.

Fess Parker "gives 'em what fer" in Disney's "Davy Crockett at the Alamo" (1955). Courtesy of Walt Disney Prod.

Reynold Brown's original sketch for *The Alamo* poster art. From the collection of Paul Andrew Hutton; courtesy of Reynold Brown.

This Disney-produced stamp for the Republic of Maldives shows a typical Davy pose in front of an Alamo clearly modeled on John Wayne's. From the author's collection.

would not have been possible without the heroic sacrifice of the men who died on that Sunday morning so long ago.

That is why people all over Texas, all over the United States, and all over the world will always remember the Alamo.

★ ★ ★

This fairly superficial account of the siege and fall of the Alamo is a relatively conservative, by-the-books version of the general story. From the viewpoint of popular culture, however, much of the foregoing amounts to revisionist heresy. Virtually no Alamo film or play has ever omitted Travis's drawing of the line, and only a couple have admitted that any Texians survived the battle and were executed later. There are *certainly* no pop-culture treatments that would even go near the suggestion that David Crockett was among these murdered prisoners. (A possible exception is Jesus Trevino's 1982 PBS production, *Seguin*. For more details on that film, please refer to Chapter Six.)

But in fact, there is very little evidence to support any of the most important events of the Alamo myth. Let's look at a few of the prominent ones.

Numbers

Elsewhere in this book, I have already addressed the issue of numbers. The *legendary* Alamo was pitifully outnumbered—180-odd defenders against thousands and thousands of Mexican soldiers. The *historical* Alamo was manned by as many as 250 men, while the attacking force was probably around 1,500. Certainly, Santa Anna's army in San Antonio during the siege may have been as large as 5,000, but not all of them attacked the Alamo that morning. Of course, 1,500 against 250 is still an unfair fight, and the result of the battle was inevitable as soon as the buglers blew attack. But it was not quite the overpowering massacre that legend would have us believe.

In mythological terms, of course, the fewer the defenders and the larger the attacking force, the greater the bravery and honor of the Alamo dead. Speaking at the site in 1842, Edward Burleson repeated a reference that was already a common element in the public's perceptions of the Alamo:

Citizens, the feeling inspired by events within these consecrat-
ed walls, of so recent date, fills my bosom with emotions. This
sacred spot, and those crumbling remains, the desecrated temple
of Texian liberty will teach a lesson which free man can never
forget. And, while we mourn the unhappy fate of Travis,
Crockett, Bowie, and their brave compatriots, let it be the boast
of Texians that though *Thermopylae had her messenger of
defeat, the Alamo had none.* [italics mine]

Within days of the battle, the Alamo defenders had already been
linked to the 300 Spartans who sacrificed themselves to the Persians'
overwhelming odds at Thermopylae in 480 B.C. On March 26, 1836,
the citizens of Nacogdoches issued this proclamation:

The tongue of every noble spirit of whom we speak is silent in
death and we anticipate in a succinct and imperfect narrative the
future Glory of their fame. They died martyrs to liberty; and on
the altar of their sacrifice will be made many a vow that shall
break the shackles of tyranny. Thermopylae is no longer without
a parallel, and when time shall consecrate the dead of the Alamo,
Travis and his companions will be named in rivalry with
Leonidas and his Spartan band.

The sentiment was simplified for the first Alamo monument in
Austin: "Thermopylae had her messenger of defeat—the Alamo had
none."

In some respects the Alamo legend, even when at odds with history,
can be inspiring and uplifting. But the issue of the numbers has been
used to further inflame the ethnic bitterness that is also a part of the
story. The implication is that the Mexicans could only have won the battle that day because they vastly outnumbered the Alamo defenders; that
is, no Mexican could beat a real American in a fair fight. This unfortunate perception has never entirely vanished. Kevin R. Young, a leading
Alamo historian, worked for a time at the Alamo IMAX Theater in San
Antonio. He introduced showings of *Alamo . . . the Price of Freedom*
(1988), and then chatted with customers in the lobby after the show.

Young told me that on many occasions, Anglo viewers would emerge from the theater and approach him with annoyance in their voices. They were peeved that the climactic battle scenes included many instances in which one Mexican soldier was shown killing one Alamo defender.

Travis's Line in the Sand

The drawing of a line in the sand is undoubtedly the most treasured incident in the Alamo myth. It is the solemn moment when the men of the Alamo consciously decide to sacrifice their lives so that Texas might live. They know that to stay in the Alamo will mean a horrible death, but they don't hesitate. Young Tapley Holland is the first to leap over the line. His hand over his heart, he cries, "I am willing to die for Texas!" The others follow. Even Jim Bowie, sick unto death, calls out, "Boys, lift my cot across that line!"

Only Louis "Moses" Rose opts out. A former Napoleonic soldier, he has already survived battles like Waterloo, and isn't willing to go down in an old mud fort in Texas. The others wish him a fond farewell, and he leaps over the wall. As he does, he sees that slaughtered Mexicans cover the ground outside the Alamo. His "wallet" [a small bag of clothes] falls into a pool of blood, which causes his clothes to stick together in the coagulated mess. Rose makes his way across the barren landscape, becoming a kind of human pincushion along the way, his legs darted with long cactus thorns. Finally, Rose arrives at the home of his old friends, the Zubers. While recuperating there, he tells them his terrible story.

Of course, and with apologies to the family of Tapley Holland, as brilliant and shining a moment of Alamo heroism as this story represents, there is almost no reason to believe it happened. First, and most important, there is the matter of just how hopeless the men of the Alamo were in the last days of the siege. The standard story is that James Butler Bonham rode bravely through the Mexican lines to deliver his dark message: "Fannin isn't coming. There will be no help."

But is that the message Bonham brought?

In 1987 historian Thomas Ricks Lindley discovered a document that changes the entire complexion of the last days of the Alamo. It is a letter to Travis from Maj. R. M. Williamson (better known as "Three-Legged Willie") dated March 1, 1836. Discovered among Travis's papers after the fall of the Alamo, it was released as a broadside in Mexico on March 31, 1836. The letter reads:

> You cannot conceive my anxiety: today it has been four whole days that we have not the slightest news relative to your danger-ous situation and we are therefore given over to a thousand con-jectures regarding you. Sixty men have left this municipality, who in all probability are with you by this date. Colonel Fannin with 300 men and four pieces of artillery has been on the march towards Béxar three days now. Tonight we await 300 reinforce-ments from Washington, Bastrop, Brazoria and S. Felipe and no time will be lost in providing you assistance. . . . P.S. For God's sake hold out until we can assist you.—I remit to you with major Bonham a communication from the interim governor. Best wishes to all your people and tell them to hold on firmly by their "wills" until I go there.—Williamson.—Write us very soon.[7]

Williamson's letter means that Bonham entered the Alamo on about March 3 with *good* news, not bad. At any time, nearly 700 men would be arriving to help Travis hold the fort. Those reinforcements and the firepower they would bring with them might just be enough to hold Santa Anna at bay indefinitely, or at least until Houston could get there with the rest of his army.

Even if Travis's joy at this news faded over the next two days, and he decided that help wasn't coming after all, would he have said so to the men? Possibly. After all, only a couple of months earlier, Ben Milam had virtually drawn his own line in the sand when he called out, "Who will come with old Ben Milam into San Antonio?" And, as most Travis-philes are fond of saying, asking his men to cross the line in the sand is the kind of dramatic gesture Travis would have loved.

But the point is, no credible evidence exists that Travis did any such thing. No Alamo survivor ever mentioned the line in the sand until after the so-called Moses Rose account surfaced in 1873, almost forty years after the fact. It does seem curious that such a moment could have slipped everyone's mind until decades later, when newspaper reporters reminded them about it. Perhaps they all really did forget about it; or perhaps they were just going along with the Alamo story of the moment by suddenly "remembering" it themselves.

The story of Moses Rose was first made public when W. P. Zuber's "An Escape from the Alamo" was published in the 1873 edition of the *Texas Almanac* (pp. 80–85). Zuber claimed that Rose had told the story to Zuber's parents, and that they in turn had passed it on to him. Thirty-five years later, Zuber wrote down what he could remember and, without apology, made up the rest. In the *Texas Almanac* piece, Zuber said:

> I wrote the sentiments of the speech in what I imagined to be Travis's style. . . . Of course, it is not pretended that Colonel Travis's speech is reported literally, but the ideas are precisely those he advanced and most of the language is also nearly the same.

Zuber later wrote in a letter dated September 14, 1877:

> I found a deficiency in the material of the speech, which from my knowledge of [Travis] I thought I could supply. I accordingly threw in one paragraph which I firmly believe to be characteristic of Travis, and without which the speech would have been incomplete.

Walter Lord, among others, speculates that the "one paragraph" that Zuber threw in was the part about the line itself.[8]

It was only after Zuber's account appeared that other Alamo survivors began mentioning the line. The highly suspect Madame Candelaria, who claimed to have nursed Jim Bowie through his final days, mentioned it for the first time in an 1899 interview. Enrique Esparza didn't talk about it until 1902. And Susanna Dickinson didn't bring it up until 1881—and she had the story reversed: Whoever wanted to *leave* should cross the line. "But one stepped out," she recalled. "His name to the best of my recollection was Ross."

Gradually the story of the line began appearing in history books and school texts, and soon it was an inextricable part of the Alamo legend. But historians have always had a hard time believing it. In fact, there isn't much to indicate that there even was a Louis Rose in the Alamo.

In 1939, R. B. Blake, an amateur historian, did a great deal of research on Rose and found many land documents in which a Louis Rose served as witness. Families of the Alamo dead were eligible for land grants if they could prove their kin had really perished there. Louis Rose lent his support whenever he could, serving as witness on several land grant applications. For instance, Blake found the application of the "Heirs of John Blair, decd." on which Rose has testified that he "left him in the Alamo 3 March 1836."[9] Blake was convinced that Rose was the real deal. But others who knew him characterized Rose as a yarn spinner. It is at least possible that he simply lied about being in the Alamo in order to testify on the grant applications—for a kickback.

And even if Rose *was* in the Alamo and left, *when* did he leave? In an article filled with suspicious elements, perhaps the most suspicious detail in Zuber's piece regards exactly when Rose went over the wall. Rose told the Zubers that he found the ground outside covered with slaughtered Mexicans, and that pools of blood were everywhere. Those who believe that Travis drew the line put the date at either March 3 (which Rose claimed) or March 5. But there would be no slaughtered Mexicans outside the walls of the Alamo on either of those dates. The possibility then arises that Rose did indeed leave the Alamo—*during* the battle. Perhaps ashamed of his cowardice, or fearful of reprisals, he might have made up the story of the line as a way to explain honorably how he came to have escaped death that morning. This, of course, is mere conjecture. Like every other element of the whole drama of the line, the facts are probably unknowable now.

That being the case, perhaps we can retain the drawing of the line as a shining mythic moment without quite claiming it as a historical reality. Without the line, the men of the Alamo have no specific moment of decision—and decision is what the legend of the Alamo is all about. The whole myth rises or falls on their deliberate choice to die. Otherwise, the battle of the Alamo is just a chaotic, bloody event of horror and death without the ennobling, quasi-religious element of willing martyrdom. Without the line, we must redefine the very meaning of the Alamo. Revisionist historians, of course, are trying to do that all the time. But those who want their legends a bit more pristine could do worse than to heed Walter Lord on this one:

> As matters stand, there's still room to speculate, and every good Texan can follow the advice of J. K. Beretta in the *Southwest Historical Quarterly*: "Is there any proof that Travis didn't draw the line? If not, then let us believe it."[10]

Versions of the capture and execution of Alamo prisoners, including Davy Crockett, are nothing new. Significantly, these stories never cast aspersions on the prisoners' character. In C. Richard Schaare's 1935 children's book, *The Life of Davy Crockett in Picture and Story,* six Texans—Crockett and Travis among them—fight until they are "so worn they could hardly stand."

Mexican General Castrillon calls upon the Alamo defenders to surrender, promising them safety. From the author's collection.

But Santa Anna, upon being informed of the promise, "flew into a rage and ordered all shot." From the author's collection.

Enraged, Crockett springs at Santa Anna with his Bowie knife and is stopped by "a dozen swords plunged into his body." From the author's collection.

In the 1952 E.C. comic, "Two-Fisted Tales," a Mexican soldier agonizes over his part in the executions. Crockett is not among them. From the author's collection.

The Execution of Survivors

If Travis's drawing of the line is the central inspiring moment of the Alamo myth, the execution of the prisoners after the battle is the dirty little secret that almost no patriotic Texan wants to know. For generations taught the inspiring line about "Thermopylae's messenger of defeat," the battle of the Alamo is all about dying to the last man. If it isn't a definitive last stand, then what is it?

Ah, what indeed?

In Alamo films, the firing always ceases as soon as the final Alamo defender has met his glorious demise. Of course, the real battle trailed off more gradually. Some of the Mexican soldiers, worked up to a fever pitch by the excitement and horror of battle, continued to fire at and mutilate the defenders' bodies long after all the Texians were dead. Fernando Urissa, Santa Anna's aide-de-camp, recalled that the blood lust was so high in the battle's aftermath that some Mexican soldiers even shot a cat they saw scurrying through the carnage. "It is not a cat," one said, "but an American."

Several Mexicans reported witnessing the execution of survivors, but the accounts vary widely. Urissa saw the murder of "a venerable old man" whom General Castrillon tried to save. Urissa recalled:

> Santa Anna replied, "What right have you to disobey my orders? I want no prisoners," and waving his hand to a file of soldiers he said, "Soldiers, shoot that man," and almost instantly he fell, pierced with a volley of balls. Castrillon turned aside with tears in his eyes . . .

Urissa asked the old man's name and was told it was "Coket."

Antonio Cruz y Arrocha, a San Antonian who lived near the Alamo, claimed that several Texians approached Santa Anna and "kneeled, each one holding a small white flag." Santa Anna saw them, made a sign to his soldiers, and "they were immediately showered by bayonet stabs."

Manuel Loranca, a Mexican lieutenant, remembered seeing the corpses of Bowie and Travis before entering a "corridor which served the Texians as quarters and here found all refugees which were left.

President Santa Anna immediately ordered that they should be shot, which was accordingly done."

Another officer, Jose Juan Sanchez Navarro, was "horrified by some cruelties, among others, the death of an old man named Cochran and a boy of about fourteen."

And another, Francisco Becerra, told of finding Travis and Crockett alive in a room "sitting on the floor among feathers." Becerra claimed that Travis offered him money to let him go, but they were both brought before Santa Anna. They were both shot and, according to Becerra, they "died undaunted, like heroes."

Ramon Martinez Caro, Santa Anna's secretary, saw five prisoners executed. He also claimed that they were protected by Castrillon, who was "severely reprimanded" by Santa Anna "for not having killed them." As Castrillon stood by, some of Santa Anna's soldiers "stepped out of their ranks, and set upon the prisoners until they were all killed."[11] But by far the most controversial report of such executions came from Jose Enrique de la Pena, a lieutenant colonel in the Zapadores battalion. De la Pena, who kept a journal throughout the Texas campaign, in later years began embellishing it with other reports. There is an ongoing controversy about the legitimacy of this document; but if it is genuine, it is one of the most valuable records of the Texas Revolution in existence.[12] De la Pena described the event this way:

> Shortly before Santa Anna's speech, an unpleasant episode had taken place which, since it occurred after the end of the skirmish, was looked upon as base murder and which contributed greatly to the coolness that was noted. Some seven men had survived the general carnage and, under the protection of General Castrillon, they were brought before Santa Anna. Among them was one of great stature, well proportioned, with regular features, in whose face there was the imprint of adversity, but in whom one also noticed a degree of resignation and nobility that did him honor. He was the naturalist David Crockett, well known in North America for his unusual adventures, who had undertaken to explore the country and who, finding himself in Béxar at the very moment of surprise, had taken refuge in the Alamo, fearing that his status as a foreigner might not be respected. Santa Anna

Susannah Dickinson is often called "the mother of the Alamo." She and her baby daughter Angelina and Travis's slave, Joe, are usually regarded as the only Alamo survivors. In fact, well over a dozen women and children lived through the siege. The number of men who survived the battle remains a mystery. From the author's collection.

Arthur Hunnicutt's Crockett is "persuaded" to give a speech upon his arrival in San Antonio in this scene from *The Last Command* (1955). Courtesy of Republic Pictures.

answered Castrillon's intervention in Crockett's behalf with a gesture of indignation and, addressing himself to the zappers, the troops closest to him, ordered his execution. The commanders and officers were outraged at this action and did not support the orders, hoping that once the fury of the moment had blown over these men would be spared; but several officers who were around the president and who, perhaps, had not been present during the moment of danger, became noteworthy by an infamous deed, surpassing the soldiers in cruelty. They thrust themselves forward, in order to flatter their commander, and with swords in hand, fell upon these unfortunate, defenseless men just as a tiger leaps upon his prey. Though tortured before they were killed, these unfortunates died without complaining and without humiliating themselves before their torturers. It was rumored that General [Ramirez y] Sesma was one of them; I will not bear witness to this, for though present, I turned away horrified in order not to witness such a barbarous scene. Do you remember, comrades, that fierce moment which struck us all with dread, which made our souls tremble, thirsting for vengeance just a few

Brian Keith (left) as Crockett and James Arness as Bowie in the television production *The Alamo: 13 Days to Glory* (1987).

moments before? Are your resolute hearts not stirred and still full of indignation against those who so ignobly dishonored their swords with blood? As for me, I confess that the very memory of it makes me tremble and that my ear can still hear the penetrating, doleful sound of the victims.

Carmen Perry's translation of this important account in 1975 won her a great deal of acclaim. But it also bought her an enormous headache. She was widely blamed for calling Davy Crockett a coward, and received angry letters and many indignant book reviews. When historian Dan Kilgore gathered all the eyewitness reports for an excellent little volume called *How Did Davy Die?*, he received even more flak—and more than one death threat.

"The Death of Bowie," an illustration by Louis Betts, was published in *McClure's Magazine*, January 1902. From the collection of Paul Andrew Hutton.

The truth is, the image of Fess Parker, swinging Ol' Betsy at the attacking Mexicans in the last moments of Walt Disney's film, *Davy Crockett at the Alamo,* is probably more responsible than any other single factor for these angry responses. Every baby boomer knows precisely how Davy Crockett died, and it wasn't after being tortured by a bunch of brown-nosing Mexican officers.

That this response is silly beyond belief should go without saying. In the decades before the Crockett craze of the fifties, stories of Crockett's capture and execution were quite common. No one seems to have taken the slightest exception to them. In C. Richard Schaare's children's book *Pioneer Stories for Boys* (New York: Cupples & Leon Co., 1934), Crockett is surrounded and persuaded by Castrillon to surrender. In good faith, he does. But when Crockett realizes that Santa Anna is going to kill him anyway, he draws his Bowie knife and springs for the dictator. "But before he could cover half the distance, a dozen swords plunged into his body. The other prisoners received the same fate." This ending neatly provides the story of Crockett being taken prisoner with a more heroically satisfying coda.

In the same year, an edition of *The Adventures of Davy Crockett, Told Mostly by Himself* (New York: Charles Scribner's Sons, 1934) told a similar story. The book even included a striking color illustration by John W. Thomason Jr. that shows a captured Crockett being brought before Santa Anna. Significantly, when the book was reprinted in the fifties, the illustration was gone.

As Paul Andrew Hutton has written, the story of Crockett's execution "was often used by the press in 1836 as further evidence of Santa Anna's barbarity . . . it was not considered to be a negative reflection on Crockett."[13] And if the de la Pena account is genuine, *it* casts no negative reflection on Crockett, either. Of all the eyewitness accounts, only Becerra's bribe story can be called insulting, and it is so transparently silly that no one would take it seriously for a moment anyway.

Although none of the accounts really match up—various eyewitnesses report one, two, five, and seven prisoners—it seems certain that at least some of the Alamo's defenders lived through the battle and were executed afterward, either by gunshot or sword. Whether Crockett was among them remains more controversial than the matter should be. No matter how he died, he certainly perished in the Alamo with all of his comrades. Irate baby boomers may object to the possibility that he may

The attack on the Alamo as seen in *Man of Conquest* (1939), a biographical film about Sam Houston. Courtesy of Republic Pictures.

have survived, or even surrendered. If so, it is they—not Jose Enrique de la Pena or Carmen Perry or Dan Kilgore—who insult Crockett when they scorn one of the Alamo's heroes for not dying correctly.

The Men Who Ran

Once again, we find ourselves in "Thermopylae had her messenger of defeat—the Alamo had none" territory. Even counting the men who were captured and executed, did all the defenders actually die in the Alamo? As it turns out, almost certainly not. At least one Texian was discovered much later in the day hiding under a bridge. A local woman doing her washing saw him and reported him to some nearby soldiers,

The aftermath of the battle from *The Last Command* (1955). Oddly, the funeral pyres are almost never a part of Alamo movies; one of the few exceptions is the IMAX film *Alamo . . . the Price of Freedom* (1988). Courtesy of Republic Pictures.

who immediately killed him. Then there is the puzzling story of Henry Warnell, who died three months later, in Port Lavacca. A sworn statement in an 1858 land claim says that he died of wounds received at the battle of the Alamo. Frustratingly, there are no other details on just how he got out of the fort, and how he made his way to the coast.

There was also Brigido Guerrero, one of the Tejano defenders of the Alamo. Confronted by Mexican soldiers during the battle, he somehow convinced them that he had been captured by the Texians and held prisoner in the Alamo. The Mexicans believed this very lucky man and let him go.

But the most shocking incident of the battle, and the one that shakes the myth of the last stand to its very foundations, is the flight of a group of men—somewhere between fifty and sixty of them—at some point late in the battle. Since none of them actually escaped, it's impossible to know if they were simply running scared, or if they saw what they believed was a clearing and just headed for it. But whether the flight was born of strategy or panic, it didn't work out well for them. Throughout the battle, lancers patrolled the perimeter of the fort, looking out for just such an action. As soon as the Texians got outside the walls, they were quickly cut down. Several Mexican officers reported the incident—Almonte, de la Pena, Loranca, Ramirez y Sesma—and they all interpreted it as an escape attempt. There doesn't seem to be any other way to look at it.

This large group of Texians was cut down near the Alameda, about where Commerce Street in San Antonio is today. One of the funeral pyres was located there, according to every report of the burnings. This would make no sense if there weren't a substantial number of enemy slain there for the Mexicans to dispose of. This funeral pyre seems to be the physical backup to the Mexican officers' testimonies.

We must remember that many details of Alamo history can never be known for certain, and that many of the things we do know will be forever clouded in mystery. So the historical revisionist is free to keep digging for new ways to view the conflict, while hero-worshipping traditionalists can bask freely in the warmth of their certainty. If Travis never drew the line, if Crockett was executed after the fighting, if sixty men ran from the fort and were killed in the fields, then our entire popular conception of the siege and fall of the Alamo changes dramatically. The actual event resembles the mythic idea even less than we once thought. But that should cause no pain to anyone. History and legend have always been two very separate things; and the more we learn about the Alamo, the greater the gulf between the two becomes. But that shouldn't change our fundamental response to the Alamo and what it means to us. The facts, even if we don't know them all, are finite—they're done. But our responses to what happened there, and our definitions of what those actions represent, are always changing, always evolving. It is still up to each one of us to decide which Alamo we want to remember.

That question became more than simply an academic or spiritual one within a few decades of the fall of the Alamo. A second battle was brewing, but this one would be of interpretation. The political upheaval it caused would not, perhaps, be as bloody as the events of 1836. But it would forever change the way in which we view those events.

From Army Headquarters to Department Store

The Alamo did not immediately fall into ruins after the battle. In fact, in just a few weeks, it was probably in better shape as a fort than it had ever been. After Santa Anna left San Antonio with most of his surviving soldiers, General Andrade was left with 1001 men to hold the town and refortify the Alamo. For over two months Andrade's men worked on the Alamo; unfortunately, they left absolutely no record of what they accomplished there. But when we consider what Green B. Jameson accomplished in half that time with a quarter of the men, Andrade's force just might have turned the Alamo into a real point of strength once again. Once Santa Anna won this war, the Alamo would remain as one of the important military bases of the area.

Of course, Santa Anna *didn't* win the war. On April 21, 1836, he was defeated by Sam Houston's force at San Jacinto, and the Texas Revolution was over the same day that the Republic of Texas was born. It took about a month for General Andrade to receive what must have been very frustrating orders—he was to destroy the fort that he had just spent sixty-five days rebuilding. This would have been a great time for Andrade to sit down and write, "we would rather die in these ditches than give them up to the enemy," but he didn't. General Andrade followed orders and tore most of the Alamo to the ground. (See Chapter Ten for the supernatural version of this story.)

When Andrade and his men left Béxar on May 24 to join the Mexican Army at Goliad, all that remained of the mission-fortress com-

Edward Everett's drawing of the Alamo church as it appeared in 1850 is generally considered to be among the most authentic views of the ruin. From the author's collection.

pound were the ruins of the Alamo church (the long cannon ramp had been burned), the building that contained the south-wall gate and a couple of rooms (later referred to as the Galera), and most of the long barracks. Along the west wall, a few ruined houses still stood. Soon, some of these were repaired and inhabited once again.

The house in the northwest corner of the compound was purchased by Samuel Maverick. Maverick was one of the original Texas revolutionaries. He had gone "with old Ben Milam into San Antonio," then served as a member of the Alamo garrison. On March 2, 1836, Maverick was sent to Washington-on-the-Brazos as one of the two delegates from the Alamo to the independence convention. He later wrote that his "desire to reside in this particular spot" [on Alamo Plaza] was "a foolish prejudice, no doubt, as I was almost a solitary escapee from the Alamo massacre."[1] Maverick and his wife Mary soon built a new two-story house on the spot, which stood at what is today near the corner of Houston Street and D Street.

But the rest of the compound continued to lie in ruins. An anonymous writer in 1905 recalled his boyhood memories of the place (he is referring to the Galera, or south-wall gate):

> It was a meeting place for owls; weeds and grass grew from the walls, and even the cacti plant decorated the tumble-down roof of the old building that flanked the church and stood across the square, forming the southern side of the quadrangle that was known as Alamo or Mission plaza.
>
> An embankment, evidently formed from the debris of the roof and dome that had fallen in many years before, reached from the front entrance up to the eastern wall that had been knocked down to some extent. In the south wall was a breach near the ground, said to have been made by Santa Ana's [sic] cannon.
>
> We boys could run up the embankment to the outer wall and on to the roof of the convent building (the long barracks)—it was a famous playground. No houses or tenements stood east or north of the fort. It commanded a plain view of the old town as it then was, confined to a few houses on South Alamo Street . . . [2]

Even the ruins of the Alamo were diminishing year by year. The locals, who needed building materials for their own homes, routinely removed wood and stone from the site. The minutes of the San Antonio City Council meeting of April 2, 1840, reported that a "Rev. Valdez desires to buy some stone from . . . the wall of the Alamo. The corporation of San Antonio agreed that there be sold him whatever he may need at four reals per cart load."[3] All over Bexar County, there may still be buildings with miscellaneous chunks of the Alamo augmenting their own walls.

But at about this same time, a huge step toward saving the Alamo—and, ironically, toward hastening its further ruin—was about to be taken. The U.S. Army was on the way.

But this army did not want to turn the Alamo back into a fort. There wasn't much left of the compound—and even when there had been, the place had never been very successful as a military base. No, someone in the U.S. Army decided that the remaining buildings of the Alamo could be remodeled and turned into an all-purpose headquarters with a supply depot, offices, storage facilities, blacksmith shop, and stables.

VIEW IN THE RUINS OF THE ALAMO.

"Never, in the world's history, had defense been more heroic· it has scarcely been equaled, save at the Pass of Thermopylæ."

Edward Everett's interior view of the Alamo church. Drawn after the debris had been removed from the building in preparation for remodeling the Alamo as a storehouse. From the author's collection.

An American volunteer named Edward Everett (1818–1903) was stationed in San Antonio in 1847 and ordered by Col. John Hardin to collect information about the local history and customs.[4] Everett was just the man for the job. Not only was he a meticulous researcher, but he was also an uncommonly gifted artist. He made sketches of the Alamo and the other San Antonio missions, as well as of other notable sites

Artist and Alamo authority Craig R. Covner compares the long barracks as it appeared at the time of the battle, after its remodeling by the U.S. Army, and as it looked in 1913 when the last of the Hugo-Schmeltzer building had been removed. Courtesy of Craig R. Covner.

---

around the area. Everett might have moved on to Mexico with his company if not for a wound received on September 11, 1847. While trying to break up a fight, Everett was shot in the leg by a drunken Texan. Left to recuperate in San Antonio, he filled his time by continuing to draw sketches and maps.

Everett became the clerk of Capt. James Harvey Ralston, the man who conceived of the idea of using the Alamo as an Army headquarters. Everett wrote:

> Captain Ralston, seeing that they could be made available at an inconsiderable expense, and having obtained permission from the quartermaster general, proceeded to put the plan in execution, and by his direction I made out plans and estimates for placing them in serviceable condition, in which my knowledge of construction became available.[5]

Everett's major project was to convert the ruins of the long barracks into a large, versatile building with plenty of space for offices, workshops, and living quarters for Everett and Ralston. It is usually believed that the Army simply built new outer walls over the original stone walls of the long barracks, but this was not the case. Only the front of the long barracks and the wall connecting the long barracks to the church were retained. Everything else was torn down, and the stones were used in construction wherever needed around the compound. Further, although the front wall of the long barracks' second story was retained, numerous additional doors and windows were cut through the stone until it resembled latticework. Later, during the "Second Battle of the Alamo," there would be much Sturm und Drang over the preservation of the long barracks, particularly the second story. But even by 1847, there was almost nothing left of it to preserve.

The south-wall gate and its adjoining rooms (together known as the Galera) were also remodeled, using southern pine, shingles, and plaster. Everett wrote that during the renovation, "many thousands of bats were unceremoniously evicted and rendered homeless, and from that time each was dependent for a lodging literally on his own hook." Everett objected to remodeling the Alamo church itself—which, he said, "we respected as an historic relic—and as such its characteristics were not marred by us." He did, however, have the interior cleared of its debris and while doing so made a grisly discovery: "several skeletons and other relics of the siege were found."[6]

Everett's desire to leave the Alamo church unmolested was not shared by others. He wrote, "I regret to see by a later engraving of this ruin, that tasteless hands have evened off the rough walls, as they were left after the siege, surmounting them with a ridiculous scroll, giving the building the appearance of the headboard of a bedstead." However, he admitted that "the care thus shown, however questionable its execution, is highly commendable, when compared with the wanton destruction with which other curious buildings in the vicinity have been visited, by relic hunters, or other vandals and iconoclasts."[7]

The "ridiculous scroll" that was added to the top of the Alamo church's façade was the work of Maj. Edwin Babbitt (1803–1881), who was made assistant quartermaster of the post of San Antonio in March 1849. It was Babbitt who worked out a lease agreement with the Catholic bishop of Texas, Jean Marie Odin, for the rental of the Alamo buildings. Despite the work done by Everett and Ralston, Babbitt believed that all of the surviving Alamo buildings should be razed and an entirely new army headquarters erected on the same spot. General Thomas S. Jesup disagreed. But then Jesup also disagreed with Everett and Ralston's view that the church should be respected as an historic structure; he believed it was just too big and strong a structure to be wasted. Jesup ordered Babbitt to turn the Alamo church into a usable building.

Babbitt, with the assistance of John Fries and the Russi Brothers Construction Company,[8] redesigned the ancient building. Since the Alamo church had no windows except the two in front, the remodelers cut several new windows into the thick limestone walls, on all four sides of the building. Two upper windows were added to the façade, and not too carefully either; the symmetry is off. When you stand facing the Alamo, the left upper window is centered over the one below it, while the right window is lined up edge to edge with the one under it. The contractors also added a peaked roof —the first roof the church had ever had—and constructed a second floor on the inside.

Because the peak of the new roof rose unattractively over the ragged top of the Alamo façade, it was obvious that something would have to be added to the structure. It seems to have been the German-born architect and stonemason John Fries who came up with the solution—the now-famous parapet or "hump," without which the Alamo would be rendered almost unrecognizable to most of the world.

How Fries came up with this particular design is not known, but Alamo authority Craig R. Covner has come up with a tantalizing theory—a theory that was born thousands of miles, and hundreds of years, from the Alamo.

At the northern end of Rome's Piazza del Popolo (or Plaza of the Poplars) stands one of the fabled gates of Rome, the Porto del Popolo. This ancient gate has its own extraordinary history: The severed head of the martyred Christian, Saint Valentine, was put on display there; its restoration in 1561 was reputedly based on sketches by Michelangelo; and when Queen Christina of Sweden abdicated her throne to convert to Catholicism, announcing that she would visit Rome to confer with the Pope, the Porta del Popolo was remodeled for the occasion by Renaissance master sculptor Gianlorenzo Bernini.

A 1745 engraving by Giuseppe Vasi of the Porta possibly depicts that

Two interior views of the Alamo church, ca. 1910. From the author's collection.

1655 visit from Queen Christina. The resemblance of the huge gate to the Alamo is inescapable; there have been pictures of the *Alamo* that look less like the Alamo than this Roman gate does.

But, is this strictly a coincidence? Maybe. We don't know that John Fries ever studied in Rome (he was only 18 when he arrived in Texas, so it seems unlikely), but it wouldn't matter much if he did. By the time he would have seen it, the Porta del Popolo had already been changed so many times that it no longer bore much resemblance to the Shrine of Texas Liberty. But, as Covner points out:

> Vasi's engravings of views of Rome and its monuments were immensely popular in the mid-eighteenth century and beyond. Visitors to Rome would purchase these individually, in portfolios, and in bound volumes as souvenirs of their "Grand Tour," not unlike the way latter-day tourists purchased postcards of the same sites.[9]

Covner further states that

> Vasi's fidelity to his subjects probably increased the value of his images to 18th and 19th century students of architecture, who all studied classical and Renaissance forms. John Fries would likely have had exposure or access to the engravings of Vasi . . . his recall of, or familiarity with this image of Porto del Popolo would have provided a sure-fire successful solution to his Alamo challenge.[10]

While Covner stresses that this is only conjecture—we do not have any word from Fries regarding his inspiration for the "hump"—it is a fascinating coincidence nonetheless. Today, of course, the feature chosen by Fries, no matter where it came from, has become the single most recognizable element of the Alamo. Although Davy Crockett and his band of brothers never saw such a thing during their brief, unpleasant tenure at the Alamo, the rest of us could identify the building from the hump alone. Not everyone likes it, though. Even as far back as 1909, there was a motion to take it off. And, as Kevin R. Young writes:

> As late as 1975, a University of Texas group also recommended

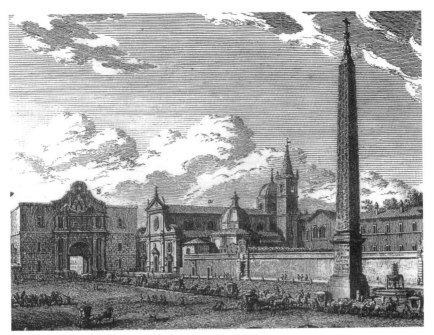

Illustration of Piazzo del Popolo

the removal of the present roof and Babbit's [sic] hump. But the official response was the same: people simply wouldn't recognize the Alamo without it.[11]

Even today, there are still Alamo purists who hate Fries's parapet and would like to see it removed. But the truth is, the Alamo has stood for a solid century and a half with the hump—longer than it ever existed without it. Fries's parapet may not have been there during the siege and fall of the Alamo, but it certainly has seen plenty of history since then.

The Alamo remained a U.S. Army depot for almost three decades—except for four years (1861–1865) when it served as Confederate headquarters. The Catholic Church, which still retained legal title to the property, attempted on several occasions to persuade the army to go away and allow the church to use the site as a school.

But by the time the Army did abandon the Alamo in 1878, the Catholic Church was no longer much interested in it. However, a local merchant, French-born Hugo Grenet, thought the place had a lot of

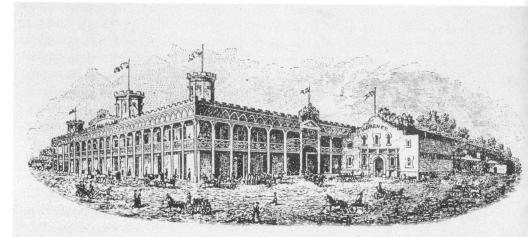

THE ALAMO AS REPAIRED BY GRENET.

The original caption of this illustration (ca. 1880) is "The Alamo as Repaired by Grenet." Actually, *repaired* might not be the operative word; *disgraced* is a little closer to the mark. From the author's collection.

promise. He offered the church $20,000 for the long barracks, which he intended to turn into a store. The church accepted Grenet's offer. The entrepreneur went to work immediately, removing much of the army remodeling from the long barracks and adding his own ornate cover to whatever scraps of wall remained. Grenet turned these historic ruins into a gaudy, two-story shopping center, offering, according to an advertisement of the time, "Groceries, Provisions, Dry Goods, Queensware, Glassware, Boots, Shoes, Whiskeys, Wines, Beers, Cigars, Tobacco, and Country Produce, second to none in the city." Mindful of the military nature of the site, Grenet had his new shopping center fronted by ornate arcades and topped off by large turrets in which he placed wooden cannon. An engraving of the period shows that he even put his name in large letters across the parapet of the church.

Not unmindful of the historic nature of the property (remember those wooden guns!), Grenet also operated a small Alamo museum inside his shopping mall. But we shouldn't infer too much respect in that gesture: Grenet also obtained a lease on the church itself and used it as a warehouse. Humorist Alexander Sweet wrote of an 1882 visit to the Alamo, where he received a tour from an "aged gentleman" who showed him all the various rooms of the Alamo in which Davy Crockett died.

"Do you see that angle in the wall, where those old cabbages and those boxes of Limberger cheese are piled? Right there at least forty Mexicans were killed. Phew, how they smell! Reckon those Limbergers must have soured! I wonder why we can't raise them right here, instead of having to import them from the North?"

"What, Mexicans?"

"No, I mean cabbages. In this room, where so much soap and axle-grease is stored, seventeen wounded Texans were shot. We have got a soap factory right here in town; we don't have to send up North for soap. 'Thermopylae had her messenger of defeat: the Alamo had none.' And it's a darned sight better article than the Yankees make, anyhow. Right here is the most sacred spot in Texas,—and it would bring sixty dollars a month if it was rented out for a saloon,—around which the sacred memories of the past cluster."[12]

A view of Alamo Plaza at the turn of the nineteenth century, showing the Alamo still attached to the Hugo-Schmeltzer building ca. 1905. From the author's collection.

Grenet's grocers didn't only keep their Limburger cheese and cabbages in the Alamo church; they also hung the carcasses of cows, pigs, and sheep there, waiting for the butcher. The bloodstains left by these unfortunate animals were regarded with patriotic awe for years afterward. One rather careless historian recalled his first visit to the Alamo:

> The interior of the building was whitewashed in 1848, but some
> of the lime had fallen away when I first visited the place in 1906,
> and stains of blood were visible, I thought. A stain was on a
> stone that projected slightly, about the height of a man's waist,
> and suggested the fancy that one of the soldiers, staggering from
> a wound, leaned against that part of the wall.[13]

Or that a future ham dinner had once hung there, curing in the cool, dark room.

Hugo Grenet died in 1882, but the long barracks' days as a shopping mall were not yet over. Another mercantile company, Hugo & Schmeltzer, bought the property for $28,000—but they weren't allowed to lease the church. The Catholic Church sold it to the state, finally yielding to feelings of patriotic pride—or perhaps they were influenced by the $20,000 check they were offered. The Right Reverend John C. Narez turned the Alamo over to the State of Texas in 1883. The City of San Antonio applied for custody and received it.

Then, in an odd turn of events, the city actually decided to concentrate on the Alamo's historic importance. To that end, workers began preparing it as a historical museum. The first thing the remodelers did was to remove the second floor that had been put there by the U.S. Army. The other changes made by the army were too drastic to undo. Now the Alamo church had large windows and a back door that had not been there during the 1836 siege. But even those who approached the place with a kind of religious awe probably didn't know or care that these anachronisms marred the historical integrity of the place. There was apparently no movement toward filling the door and windows back in—after all, even a shrine needs a little sunlight.

The State of Texas took over the property at just the right moment. The Alamo's image was due for a change. Derogatory jabs such as those in Alex Sweet's column were highly annoying to patriotic Texans, who believed that the sacred site should be accorded far more respect. San

A panel from Jack Jackson's *Los Tejanos* (1979) shows an old San Antonian bitterly contemplating what has happened to the Alamo. Courtesy of Jack Jackson.

Antonio's first railroad came onto the scene in 1877. More tourists were arriving all the time, most of them anxious to see the Alamo, so glorious in history. Nearly everyone was at least disappointed—and at most revolted—by the reality of the place, with its gaudy shopping structure on one side and its saloons and low-class shops on the other.

But there were San Antonians who were ready to give the Alamo the respect, and the setting, it deserved. These well-meaning people were about to embark on a momentous journey, fueled by ignorance and enthusiasm, leading to a minor social cataclysm that would pit friend against friend and patriot against patriot.

It would be known as the Second Battle of the Alamo.

The Second Battle of the Alamo

ow that the Alamo church was back in the hands of Texas, and no longer serving as a grocery warehouse, many Texans believed that the battle had been won. But Adina de Zavala knew the fight was far from over. De Zavala (1861–1955) was the granddaughter of Lorenzo de Zavala, one of the signers of the Declaration of Texan Independence. She had grown up with a fierce pride in Texas and a passion for the state's history. In 1889 she started meeting with a group of women to discuss historical subjects. She called the group the De Zavala Daughters. In 1891, another, similar group formed, composed entirely of female descendants of pioneers who had come to Texas before it entered the United States. That group was called Daughters of the Republic of Texas. The two groups coexisted for two years, finally joining forces in 1893. The De Zavala Daughters then became the De Zavala Chapter of the DRT.

By the time de Zavala and her group became a part of the DRT, she was already at work trying to save the Alamo. But when Adina de Zavala said "Alamo," she didn't just mean the church. She meant all surviving structures of the original mission compound:

> Only two of the buildings of the Alamo still stand, the Alamo proper, where the heroes died and piled the enemy before them in heaps, where the floor was shoe deep in the blood of friend and foe; and the old Church, then a ruin, whose north rooms

Adina de Zavala wanted to save the two-story long barracks, which she considered the true relic of the battle of the Alamo. From the author's collection.

sheltered the women and children and magazines, and which was defended by a few gunners and sharp-shooters."[1]

But there was the matter of how the rest of San Antonio saw the long barracks. Still covered by the wooden walls and rather gaudy decorations of the Hugo & Schmeltzer Mercantile Company, the structure seemed to entirely lack the dignity associated with a venerated historic shrine. To most people, it was simply an eyesore. But Adina de Zavala knew that the original walls of the mission *convento* were concealed beneath the shopping center, and she wanted to save it.

In 1892, she began to lay siege to Gustav Schmeltzer, co-owner of the enterprise. Impressed with de Zavala's zeal, Schmeltzer finally promised her "not to sell or offer the property to anyone else without notifying her, and giving the [de Zavala] chapter the opportunity to acquire it, to save it to the people of Texas, to be utilized as a Hall of Fame and Museum of History, Art, Literature and Relics."[2]

In 1900, Hugo & Schmeltzer agreed to sell. They pledged to lower their price by $10,000, which would be their gift to the Daughters. All they would require from Adina de Zavala and her society was $75,000. Although the sum didn't seem like much, especially to purchase such a crucial piece of Texas history, it was more than the Daughters as an institution could come up with. But one of the Daughters, as an individual, would have no problem writing a check for such a sum. Her name was Clara Driscoll.

Driscoll (1881–1945) had two grandfathers who had fought for the Republic of Texas, which gave her a place of honor in the DRT. And her father was a multimillionaire rancher, which gave Driscoll a place of honor just about everywhere else. She had been educated in New York and in Europe and had acquired an interest in historic preservation. Returning to Texas, she was appalled by the state of ill repair that defined most of the state's most important historic buildings.

Driscoll was especially incensed at the treatment of the Alamo. In 1900, she wrote a stinging letter to the *San Antonio Express* bemoaning the Alamo's wretched state:

> Our Alamo. . . . how do we treat it? We leave it hemmed in
> on one side by a hideous barracks-like looking building, and on
> the other by two saloons. . . . Today the Alamo should stand out

Clara Driscoll wanted to tear down the long barracks in order to emphasize the Alamo church, which *she* considered the real deal. Ultimately, Driscoll emerged (slightly) victorious. The Alamo as it exists today would be more to Driscoll's liking than to de Zavala's. From the author's collection.

free and clear. All the unsightly obstructions that hide it away should be torn down and the space utilized for a park. I am sure that if this matter were taken up by some enterprising, patriotic Texan, a sufficient amount could be raised that would enable something of this kind to be done.[3]

In this letter Driscoll made clear the fundamental difference in how she viewed the Alamo, and how Adina de Zavala viewed it. Driscoll's "hemmed in" Alamo is clearly the church only. The "hideous barracks-like building"—the Hugo & Schmeltzer company—was not historic in itself, but merely a blot that should be removed.

Driscoll even managed to bring up that blot in her short story, "The Custodian of the Alamo." In the story, a beautiful young DRT member is showing a handsome railroad tycoon around the Alamo. "Davy Crockett fell outside in the court-yard," the girl went on. "That old building outside is soon to be cleared away and a fitting surrounding given this chapel. The State has just recently purchased the property. It was through the efforts of patriotic women that it was saved for historic purposes."[4]

At first, two of those "patriotic women" were staunch allies. With the Daughters' option on the Hugo & Schmeltzer building due to expire, plans were being made to tear down the store, which included the long barracks, and build a luxury hotel there. The two women were out-raged, but for slightly different reasons: de Zavala didn't want a historic building razed; Driscoll didn't want a large building continuing to block the view of "the Alamo."

Driscoll and de Zavala met with Charles Hugo, who accepted $500 from Driscoll for a thirty-day extension on the DRT's option. At the end of that month, Driscoll wrote an even larger check for $3,478.25, which would extend the option until February 10, 1904. Over the following months, various chapters of the DRT held fund-raising activities trying to raise $20,000, which would complete the down payment. But they were able to come up with only $7,000. Once again, Clara Driscoll came to the rescue. She bought the long barracks herself, in her own name (she was later reimbursed by the State of Texas).

But while the DRT continued to search for the money to pay Driscoll back and take control of the Alamo property themselves, the ideologi-cal rift between the Driscoll and de Zavala factions continued to widen.

The long barracks (left) in about 1910, still covered by some of the Hugo-Schmeltzer building, although many of the more ornate elements have already been removed. From the author's collection.

Driscoll wrote in the *Fort Worth Record* (January 22, 1905) that the church was the only original mission building still standing: "The monastery fell to pieces long ago, and on the ground it occupied a grocery store stands today."

The transfer of the deed from Hugo & Schmeltzer to the DRT was completed in August 1905. By that time Driscoll's chapter and de Zavala's chapter were engaging in open warfare, fighting desperately for control of the Alamo. Each side celebrated its victories: Driscoll was given custody of the Alamo by the DRT executive committee, but de Zavala was given custodianship of the site by the city. Friends of Driscoll's tried to change the locks to keep de Zavala and her cohorts out, but de Zavala "soon arrived upon the scene, relieved the locksmith

A song to celebrate Adina de Zavala's efforts to save the Alamo. Sales of this sheet music raised funds for the De Zavala Chapter of the DRT. From the author's collection.

In 1910, according to Clara Driscoll, "The Alamo" was still "hemmed in on one side by a hideous barracks-like building." But that was soon to change. From the Coppini collection, DRT Library.

of his lock and tools and put him ignominiously to flight."[5] Infuriated, the Driscollites "seceded" and formed the Alamo Mission Chapter on April 18, 1906.

When a hotel firm bought property just east of the Alamo in 1907 and planned to erect a $500,000 luxury hotel there, the controversy grew even more intense. The Vanderventer Hotel Company asked the DRT to approve the razing of the Hugo & Schmeltzer building to "make a park around the Alamo Chapel . . . and further offered to pay the salary of a Custodian for the Alamo Chapel for a term of five years."[6] When de Zavala protested to Charles M. Reeves of St. Louis, the man who was making the purchase on behalf of Vanderventer, he replied with just the right tone of condescension—guaranteed to spur de Zavala into even more determined action. She had described her hope of turning the long barracks into a Hall of Fame. Reeves wrote that such a thing

cannot add to, but necessarily detract from, the thing well done. [Your] position is historically incorrect. At the time of the battle of the Alamo only the south wall of the Mission was standing. Texas patriots wish to preserve only that which has to do with

In 1911, the last remnants of the Hugo-Schmeltzer building were torn away, leaving only the skeletal remains of the long barracks. *Above*: From the Coppini collection, DRT Library. *Below*: From the DRT Library

Adina de Zavala's bitter fight to save the second story of the long barracks was doomed to failure. One good reason, as this 1911 view shows, is that there wasn't much second story left to save. From the author's collection.

her history . . .

What you propose to do in the perpetuation of the walls of this old building would simply result in preserving indefinitely an eye-sore which would be a source of humiliation and regret to the people of San Antonio for all time.[7]

The Driscoll faction was highly in favor of the hotel proposal. The hotel would be set far enough back behind the Alamo that it wouldn't detract from any of the church's sight lines. And with the financial bonanza from such a deal, a beautiful park could be designed and sustained—which is precisely what Driscoll wanted.

The De Zavala Chapter, along with local businessmen, helped to quash the hotel plans, but the long barracks weren't out of danger yet. Adina de Zavala began to believe that the only way to take control of the entire remaining Alamo mission was to *seize* control of it—by force, if necessary. On February 10, 1908, as the sheriff and other officials tried to serve de Zavala with an injunction against her occupying the

The Alamo stood beside the ruins of the long barracks for nearly two years, until the upper story—what was left of it—was finally removed under the orders of Lt. Governor Will Mayes. From the author's collection.

premises, she darted inside the abandoned Hugh & Schmeltzer building, locked all the doors, and barricaded herself inside. The guerilla action made headlines all over the United States, giving unprecedented publicity to de Zavala's fight to save the Alamo. She stayed inside for three days and nights. Although the story was put out that she was refused food and water, in fact, her supporters kept her comfortable throughout her demonstration.

Though she seemed to emerge from the long barracks victorious, ultimately de Zavala's gesture was futile. In 1911, Governor Colquitt agreed with the De Zavala Chapter that every existing wall of the original mission should remain standing. The wooden walls and other outer structure of the Hugo & Schmeltzer building were soon removed, leaving only the vulnerable old stone walls standing. But even though the Driscoll faction was reconciled to keeping the long barracks standing, they wanted to take off what was left of the second floor to give a better view of the church. Colquitt adamantly refused to give his permission to do so, but when he was out of the state in 1913, Lt. Gov. Will Mayes ordered the demolition of the upper story.

The irony is that both Driscoll and de Zavala were coming at the controversy from the wrong direction, operating out of ignorance of what the original Alamo mission was really like. Adina's conceptual art of her proposed reconstructed long barracks shows a mighty two-story building, fronted with elaborate arcades. In fact, her conception of the "original" mission didn't look all that different from the Hugo & Schmeltzer building. In the drawing, the Alamo church stands humbly off to the side, clearly subordinate.

The Alamo in 1918. By this time, a new back wall had been constructed for the long barracks, with the hopes of rebuilding it for a museum. This reconstruction never happened. The structure remained roofless until 1968. Today, it houses the Long Barracks Museum. From the author's collection.

But the long barracks didn't exist under the Hugo & Schmeltzer building; only the front wall of the long barracks still stood. And the bitterly contested upper story was nothing more than a Swiss cheese of stone, with numerous doors and windows cut through the original wall. There was an attempt to reconstruct the long barracks, but the back wall and the arcade beyond it had to be rebuilt out of the stone that had been knocked off the second story. Today, the long barracks houses the Alamo's museum—much as Adina de Zavala hoped it would—but visitors who believe they are standing in an original Alamo structure are mistaken. It is an almost total reconstruction.

Clara Driscoll clearly won the second battle of the Alamo. Not only is she widely remembered today as the "Savior of the Alamo," but she is the architect behind what stands there now. It is Clara Driscoll's ideal Alamo that visitors see today.

Adina de Zavala was, in her way, just as wrongheaded as Driscoll. She had a bizarre idea of what the original long barracks looked like, and her plan to deemphasize what was clearly the most interesting and eye-catching building on the compound was a mistake. From the beginning, even while much more of the compound stood—including the south wall and gate—people always thought of the church as "The Alamo." Then as now, it was a clear victory of image over history. That, of course, pretty much defines almost all aspects of the Alamo right down the line.

The Alamo of Poet and Playwright

A battle may not be written in verse!
And prose, sometimes, is even worse.

> Morton Simms Watts
> *The Maid of the Alamo or the*
> *Incarnation of Chivalry* (1913)

In many ways, the age in which the Alamo fell was a far more literate—or, at least, more literary—one than our own. The written word was a primary source of news, entertainment, and personal communication. Perhaps fewer people, proportionate to the population, could read or write, but those who could generally showed a mastery of language and imagery that puts the modern letter-writer to shame.

It was also a time when news reporters were given a great deal more leeway than today, not only in which facts they would present but also in how they would present those facts. The newspapers of the day are filled with casual editorializing within otherwise straightforward news stories that would get a reporter fired today.

The Poems

And it seemed that everyone who could write at all was automatically a poet. Publications of 1836—newspapers, magazines, brochures—are simply dripping with poetry. As Philip Graham writes:

Schools and libraries were almost entirely lacking during the days of the Republic [of Texas]. But the literary spark was kept alive by the [newspaper] editors, a tribe of versatile and brave men. . . . Each paper boasted a "Poet's Corner," filled with either naïve or borrowed compositions. A single issue of *The Texas Republic* (Brazoria) printed five poems. [Most of the] other leading papers of the Republic usually printed from one to four poems in each issue.[1]

And so it isn't surprising that the first responses to the fall of the Alamo—indeed, the first *reports* of the fall—came in the form of poetry, like this angry bit from the *New Orleans Commercial Bulletin*:

Vengeance on Santa Anna and his minions,
Vile scum, up boiled from the infernal regions,
Dragons of fire on black sulphuros pinions,
The offscouring baseness of hell's blackest legions,
Too filthy far with crawling worms to dwell
And far too horrid and too base for hell.

There is, in fact, a virtual rhyming history of the Texas Revolution for anyone who has the patience to seek out all the poems—and the stomach to read some of them. Mirabeau B. Lamar seems to yearn for the approaching trouble in his 1835 poem, "The Bride That I Woo Is Danger."

When shall I meet the audacious foe,
Face to face where the flags are flying?
I long to thin them, "two at a blow,"
And ride o'er the dead and the dying!

And H. Kerr thumbed his nose at Santa Anna in "New Yankee Doodle," published in October 1835:

Santa Anna did a notion take, that he must rule the land, sir;
The church and he forthwith agree to publish the command, sir.
In Mexico none shall be free—

See the Stirring....

DRAMA OF THE ALAMO

"A CLOUD OF WITNESSES"

MISSION SAN JOSE
OUTDOOR THEATRE
HIGHWAY 281-S
SAN ANTONIO, TEXAS

WITH A CAST
OF 60
NIGHTLY DURING JULY
(Except Monday Nites)
Gates Open at 6:30 P.M.
for Fiesta Foods ---
Show Starts at 8:15 P.M.

TICKETS AVAILABLE AT—Municipal Auditorium, The Alamo, Gunter Hotel or San Antonio Conservation Society — CA 3-5122
$1.50 & $2.00 (Children Under 12—75c in $1.50 Section)

From the author's collection.

The people are too blind to see;
They cannot share the liberty
Of Yankee Doodle Dandy.

And, yes, it's supposed to be sung to the tune to "Yankee Doodle Dandy"—but it takes a little creativity to cram all the words in.

The first blood of the Texas Revolution was celebrated in verse ("Brave Ben Milam"), as were numerous angry calls to arms: "Texians, To Your Banner Fly," "To Santa Anna," "War Song," and "The Texian War Cry." It is in this latter poem that we find one of the first poetic references to the Alamo:

And by that blood-stained altar kneeling,
The scathed and war-torn Alamo,
We pledge all of our patriot feeling
To hurl red vengeance on the foe.

Reuben Potter, one of the first Alamo historians, wrote "Hymn of the Alamo," which was published on October 4, 1836. In this verse, he uses imagery that had already become an irrevocable part of Alamo mythology:

Here on this new Thermopylae,
Our monument shall tower on high
And Alamo hereafter be
In bloodier fields the battle cry.

Perhaps most famous of all was the benediction on the Alamo dead, published in April 1836 in the *Telegraph and Texas Register*. It isn't a poem, but is written in the poetic style so common in the era:

Spirits of the mighty, though fallen! Honors and rest are with ye: the spark of immortality which animated your forms shall brighten into a flame, and Texas, the whole world, shall hail ye like the demi-Gods of old, as founders of new actions, and as patterns of imitation!"

As time passed, the Alamo of poetry became less of a watchword for vengeance and more a revered symbol of freedom. But no matter what the approach, the poet always reserved considerable license for the telling of the tale. In his foreword to *Siege of the Alamo: A Mexico-Texan Tale* (1888), William S. Heavenhill wrote this slightly apologetic explanation:

> It is needless to say, that I have not adhered strictly to the history of the Alamo in writing this poem. This fact all readers suffi-ciently acquainted with its history will observe. While the siege actually lasted eleven days, here it occupies only two. Had I cele-brated the full number of days, it would have been necessary, in my opinion, to have written a poem with eleven parts, devoting one part to each day, and to do this it would indeed have required the pen of a Virgil or a Homer to accomplish successfully.[2]

In the appendix Heavenhill writes, still a bit apologetically, "I am aware that Santa Anna commanded the Mexican army in person in this Siege; but I have given Almonte, one of his generals, that place, as his name is more suited to the meter."[3] If only all Alamo authors, poets, playwrights, and filmmakers were this honest—history is one thing, rhythm quite another!

In 1913, Morton Simms Watts published a tiny volume of poetry called *The Maid of the Alamo or The Incarnation of Chivalry.* It seemed to Watts at the time that the heroic deeds of historic Texans were in dan-ger of being forgotten, even in Texas. "Do not [Texas's] heroes and statesmen compare with those that have lived in any age or country?" Watts wrote. "Are there any names in historic or legendary lore that deserve to be written higher on the white-roll of Fame than the founders of Texas? It is certain that no well-informed Texan thinks so."

Watts's poem is alternately confusing, haunting, silly, and passionate. Sometimes he just seems to be marking time, as when he tries to think of something to say about Sam Houston:

He was the commander-in-Chief
And was seeking to give relief
To Travis in the Alamo,
Besieged by troops of Mexico.

And sometimes he actually conjures up an image of some power:

A woman walks alone in the court
In a pool of blood slips her foot;
Falling on her hands and knees
An unsheathed sword she near her sees;
Quick, within her shawl she folds it
And, a priceless prize she holds it.

As over the court morning steals
Travis' face the light reveals,
His fine features, now calm and fair
Are shaded by a lock of hair,
Still wet and warm with his rich blood;
A long knife she drew from her belt,
Its keen edge with her thumb she felt –
As by his side she meekly knelt.

Then from his brow the lock she clipt,
And in her vest the token slipt.

Watts wasn't much of a poet, but the published version of his poem is worth owning by the Alamo-phile with an appreciation for the sublimely ridiculous. *The Maid of the Alamo* is illustrated by six photographs, taken especially for this book. The photographs have obviously been staged in someone's back yard, using friends and neighbors who were apparently left to their own devices regarding costumes, which range from Civil War issue to 1913-era street clothes. But it's the location of the photos that makes them so wonderful. The photographer saw absolutely no reason to disguise where they were, or to even attempt to approximate San Antonio of 1836. Consequently, the lock-clipping scene from above is pictured on a nice lawn with a white picket fence in the background and a nice suburban neighborhood plainly on view behind the fence.

Evelyn Brogan's 1922 poem, *James Bowie, a Hero of the Alamo,* lacks the giddy nonsense of Morton Simms Watts's poem, so it is better as poetry without being quite so entertainingly silly. Brogan wrote her poem with serious history in mind, filling the slim volume not only with

"Now Opening Wide Her Glaring Eyes." Although you wouldn't know it to look at it, this scene from Morton Simms Watts's "The Maid of the Alamo" is supposed to take place in Santa Anna's tent. Yes, these guys are supposed to be Mexican officers. The woman is a witch or something. From the author's collection.

---

the work itself, but with a historical foreword. As an appendix to the book, Brogan included a pretty impressive selection of Alamo-related letters and documents. These include not only Travis's famous "We are besieged" letter but also the marriage record of Bowie and Ursula Veramendi, as well as an 1881 interview with Susannah Dickinson.

Brogan tells the story of the Alamo briskly and emotionally through her poem, managing to work an astonishing amount of detail into what is obviously a very well-researched work. She is even a talented enough poet to take on a famous document and mold it into her poem's particular rhythms:

. . . the plea
Travis sends is an urgent one. "We
Beg you to come and assist us here
For we are surrounded by men who fear

Neither God nor man, and help we must have
If victory be ours. You may salve
Your conscience and refuse to hear
Our urgent call, but never fear
Though we be neglected, I will sustain
Myself, or die like a soldier who has lain
Down his life for his country and his own honor.
Victory or Death!"

Any discussion of Alamo poetry must inevitably veer into the territory of Alamo songs. Chapter Seven includes a discussion of some Alamo songs—like "The Ballad of Davy Crockett" (1955) and "Ballad of the Alamo" (1960)—that burrowed deeply into the pop culture imaginations of the younger generation. But in the period before World War II, Alamo songs were aimed at a very different audience than the baby boomers of the fifties and sixties who responded so strongly to those bouncy *ballads*. Some of these earlier songs were martial airs, which called upon the memory of the Alamo as a symbol of vengeance, such as "Somewhere in Mexico (Remember the Alamo)." This puerile, and rather nasty, little ditty was composed in 1916 by Francis J. Lowe to "inspire" American soldiers on duty in Mexico:

Somewhere in Mexico, Remember the Alamo
Our boys so brave and true
Are hiking two by two
The army and Navy forever
Three cheers for the Red, White and Blue
You bet your life, they'll set things right
And show some Greasers how to fight,
Down in Mexico.

Not all Alamo songs were racist, of course. In fact, some simply evoked the image of the Alamo for more romantic purposes, as in Eileen Pike's "Alamo Serenade" (1938), which croons

There is only joy and peace
All your troubles seem to cease
And you find romance in a glance by the Alamo.

But most Alamo songwriters seemed to prefer restating the accepted themes of blood sacrifice. The 1895 "patriotic song and chorus" titled "The Alamo: In Memory of the Fallen Heroes of Texas" (words by Mrs. Jennie Myers, Music by Miss Ella Rodeffer) fairly wallows in dark, foreboding imagery:

A grim scarred spectre she seems as she stands
Backward she's pointing with blood stain'd hands
Back to the sepulchral black veil'd age
Whose record burns as with fire the page
As she pencils the deeds of the martyrs brave
Who died the freedom of Texas to save
Whil'st surged the Mexicans to and fro
Our brave sons guarded the Alamo

On Sunday morn March the sixth, at three
The "Deguello" sounded the death decree;
The blood-thirsting host sprang quick to arms
Shrilly the bugle pealed loud alarms
Nerved for fierce conflict our heroes stood
United by bonds of fond brotherhood
Mad waved the flag on San Fernando,
Madder they fought at the Alamo.

But the chorus urges the listener to respond to this dark tale with the tribute it deserves:

Arouse, loyal Texans a monument build
to tow'r above heroes who
battling were kill'd
struggled they bravely
in darkness and gloom
erect a monument over their tomb.

Jenny Lind Porter, once poet laureate of Texas (1964–1965) contributed one of the better latter-day Alamo poems with her "unabashedly old-fashioned, romantic narrative poem," *The Siege of the Alamo*. Begun in 1957, it wasn't published until 1981. In the interim, because

"Then from His Brow the Lock She Clipped." This plate from "The Maid of the Alamo" (1913) brings all the tragedy of the Alamo into someone's back yard. Literally. From the author's collection.

"by nature it lent itself to public readings," Porter often performed excerpts from the poem, accompanied by composer-guitarist Joseph Castle. The poem does indeed benefit from being read aloud; Porter found distinctive rhythms for each of its sections, and some parts even call for music.[4]

Porter researched her poem by reading Amelia Williams's doctoral dissertation, *A Critical Study of the Siege of the Alamo and of the Personnel of its Defenders,* which has been making life difficult for Alamo researchers since 1931. She also read John Myers's *The Alamo* (1948), A. Galand Adair and M. H. Crockett's *Heroes of the Alamo* (1956), and similar mainstream works—and, indeed, her *Siege of the Alamo* unblinkingly characterizes the entire enterprise as noble, self-sacrificial, patriotic, and heroic. This is not, in short, a revisionist's Alamo.

It is an uncommonly beautiful one, though. After wading through so much dreadful poetry on the subject, it's a genuine pleasure to come upon a work written with this kind of imagery and insight:

Before the dawn, lulled in a grateful sleep,
The Texans lay exhausted by their guns,

Worn by the days of constant, bitter siege,
Fatigue apparent on the blue young lips
And in the cheeks that hollowed strangely old
And in the hands that nerveless curled around
Their muskets through a habit of the mind
Enrique Esparza was then fast asleep
And did not mark the punctual chanticleer
Wasting his rhetoric on the numbskull hens.
There Travis lay, sleeping and waking cold,
Keeping the post which had become his world,
Sleep drowsing on the fingers which would hold
Never again the fingers of his child.

Jenny Lind Porter's poem captured the spirit of her Alamo by weaving fantasy with history in order to find an essential truth that is not always apparent in the dry facts. Michael Lind, with his 1997 *The Alamo: An Epic,* had even bigger fish to fry. It was his aim to recast the story of the Alamo, as the title suggests, as an epic along the lines of *The Odyssey,* "not in the *style* of Homer but in the *tradition* of Homer."[5] Lind completed *The Alamo* over the course of twelve years, and chose to tell a rather traditional version of the story. He wrote:

I have followed history closely although in the interest of drama or clarity I have occasionally employed the accepted devices of historical fiction, such as the omission of insignificant detail and the invention of minor scenes. In choosing between varying accounts of what happened at the Alamo, I have used plausibility, not dramatic value, as criterion.[6]

Lind elected not to include Travis's line in the sand, because "it almost certainly never happened … Aristotle thought that, in poetry, a probable impossibility was preferable to an improbable possibility. The story of Travis's line in the dust is an improbable impossibility."[7]

On the other hand, Lind chose to depict Crockett's death in combat; he doesn't believe in the veracity of de la Pena or other Mexican witnesses who claimed to see Crockett executed after the fight.

A saber scraped his temple, metal caught
his shoulder, sewing in hot agony.
Instinctively, he raised his arms, he sought
to shield his stinging face, permitting three
more bayonets to bite. Strength fled his knee,
then darkness fell before the old stone arch
at dawn on Sunday the sixth of March.

But even as he depicts Crockett's death in a more or less traditional fashion, Lind acknowledges the cutting edge of Alamo scholarship when he has several Texans run from the fort and die on the ground outside.

John Thomson fell outside the walls, and so
did Robert Campbell. John E. Gaston tried
to grab an orphaned horse, but was too slow;
like hatcheting upon a mountainside
the sound of stocks that drummed him till he died.
Another fugitive was screened by sparks
when he crashed in a campfire, William Parks.

One of the most impressive aspects of Lind's poem is that he mentions virtually every defender of the Alamo by name, a feat virtually unique in dramatized versions of the Alamo story. The battle, in Lind's hands, takes on an entirely different character because of this device. For even if Lind has invented the methods of their deaths, to spend a moment with Joshua Smith or Bill Linn or Charles Clark gives the conflict a personal, vulnerable face that nearly every poet and dramatist has missed. Lind has given faces and voices to names that otherwise live on only in dry lists, or carved in cold marble.

Undoubtedly, more Alamo poetry will be written. Indeed, if history has taught us anything, it's that there will undoubtedly be more *bad* Alamo poetry. With luck, though, there will also be more daring and thoughtful works like Michael Lind's *The Alamo: An Epic*. However, it doesn't seem very likely. Lind has raised the bar so high that it will be something like a miracle if another poet produces another work of art on the subject as comprehensive, as moving, and as beautiful.

Theatrical Works

On the evening of March 1, 1878, the curtains of the Austin Opera House rose to reveal onstage a rustic scene: a tranquil forest clearing and a small cottage made of logs. As the offstage chorus sang . . .

When high o'er the mountain
Field, valley and crag,
The sun gilds the fountain
We watch for the stag.

. . . many in the audience must have settled in for a pleasantly familiar experience. It was a production of Frank Hitchcock Murdock's famous play, *Davy Crockett, Or, Be Sure You're Right, Then Go Ahead*, starring Frank Mayo. Murdock had written the frontier melodrama specifically for Mayo, who first performed it in Rochester, New York, on September 23, 1872. In the six intervening years, Mayo had presented the play many, many times, all over the United States. No doubt many of the more cosmopolitan members of the Austin audience had seen it before. And they would have plenty of opportunities to see it again—Mayo would tour the world almost nonstop with the play, right up to his death in 1896. In fact, Mayo performed at the Broadway Theatre in Denver, Colorado, on June 6—just two days before he died. He is said to have kept count of the number of his performances until he reached two thousand—and then simply lost track.

But in at least one regard, this 1878 production of *Davy Crockett* was unlike any others. The evening's guest of honor was 64-year-old Susannah Hannig, the wife of a local cabinetmaker. In 1878, Mrs. Hannig was living a life of relative comfort and serenity; but forty-two years earlier, she had lived through an experience of the sheerest horror. As the wife, then widow, of officer Almeron Dickinson, Susannah had survived the battle of the Alamo with her baby daughter, Angelina.

Consequently, Mrs. Hannig was very probably the only person in the audience who had actually known the real Davy Crockett. She was most certainly the only one who had seen his mutilated remains in the hellish aftermath of the battle.

DEDICATED TO COMPANY E, CHARLES CITY, FIRST REGIMENT IOWA NATIONAL GUARD

SOMEWHERE IN MEXICO REMEMBER THE ALAMO

WORDS AND MUSIC
BY
Francis J. Lowe
ARRANGED BY
E. L. Jaco
Mailed on receipt of price, 25¢ in stamps to
Francis J. Lowe, Charles City, Iowa, U.S.A.
On sale at Border exclusively by
South Texas Music Company, San Antonio, Texas

From the author's collection.

Although a newspaper report tells us that the Austin Opera House had its "largest crowd ever" that night, Susannah Hannig did not go on record with her response to the play. The event might have been a slightly ghoulish one, conjuring up nightmarish images of the most terrible hours of her life. But more probably, the play had so little connection to the actual Davy Crockett that it inspired no associations in her mind at all. She may have simply enjoyed it as a rustic comedy with no further emotional reverberations.

There is something enduringly odd and fascinating about such moments, when fact and fancy meet face to face. In 1911 Enrique Esparza, who as a child saw his father die in the Alamo, still lived in San Antonio at the same time that Gaston Melies's Star Film Company was producing the first motion picture about the event—*The Immortal Alamo*. We don't know if Esparza was aware of the film; but there is at least the possibly that he saw it, thus watching the most traumatic and horrifying event of his existence turned into fifteen minutes of rousing screen melodrama. Succeeding generations turned the Alamo and its defenders into icons and legends, just as other historic events have become mythologized over the years, but the process is usually divorced from the first-hand experience. We can only wonder how, or if, Susannah Hannig or Enrique Esparza reconciled the two seemingly irreconcilable aspects of this experience.

Susannah Hannig was not the only member of the Alamo garrison to have attended a play about Davy Crockett. Davy Crockett did, too—at least, in a way.

In 1830 the American actor James Hackett put the word out that he wanted a new play, depicting a character who was distinctly American in flavor and whose dialogue reflected the amusingly grotesque jargon of a spirited but illiterate pioneer. Playwright James Kirke Paulding (later to become secretary of the navy) responded with an uproarious frontier comedy called *The Lion of the West*, which debuted in April 1831. In writing it, Paulding had contacted a friend, the painter John Wesley Jarvis, and asked for examples of "Kentucky or Tennessee manners, and especially some of their peculiar phrases & comparisons. If you can add, or *invent* a few ludicrous Scenes of Col. Crockett at Washington, You will be sure of my everlasting gratitude."[8]

The lead character of Paulding's play made good use of those "peculiar phrases and comparisons." Named Colonel Nimrod Wildfire, he was a buckskin-clad cavalier who wore a cap made of wildcat fur. He was highly capable and intelligent but conducted himself like a boor and a buffoon, much to the consternation of the very proper Mrs. Wollope. In Michael A. Lofaro's *Davy Crockett: The Man, The Legend, The Legacy, 178–1986* Richard Boyd Hauck writes:

> Wildfire's manners are in fact atrocious. Everything he does is slapstick comedy. In Mrs. Wollope's presence, he flops himself down in one chair and puts his feet up in the other, blocking her

attempt to sit; he gets roaring drunk and brags about it; he thinks his ostentatious dispensation of dollars can solve any problem.[9]

Both Paulding and Hackett denied that the uncouth character was based upon then-Congressman David Crockett—despite Paulding's direct appeal to his friends for Crockett anecdotes. But the public knew better. Although he was at first offended by it, even Crockett acknowledged his connection to the character, when the play's popularity began to be accompanied by a rise in his own. Already known as a plain-speaking backwoodsman—a character he played up with all his politician's wiles—Crockett began to take on the characteristics of Nimrod Wildfire in public life. Almost certainly, he began wearing the buckskins and fur hats by which we now identify him only *after* the play—and the Wildfire image—became popular. The Wildfire image on the posters for the play later became adapted into a Crockett portrait. And some of Wildfire's bombastic bragging was appropriated for the Crockett book, *Sketches and Eccentricities of Colonel David Crockett of West Tennessee* (1833).

In the play, Wildfire refers to himself as "half horse, half alligator," a common frontier brag, according to Richard Boyd Hauck.[10] In one scene, Wildfire meets a stranger who tells him, "I can whip my weight in wildcats."

Wildfire replies, "My father can whip the best man in old Kaintuck, and I can whip my father. When I'm good-natured I weigh about a hundred and seventy, but when I'm mad, I weigh a ton."

Davy Crockett says, in *Sketches and Eccentricities*:

I'm . . . half-horse, half-alligator, a little touched with the snapping turtle; can wade the Mississippi, leap the Ohio, ride upon a streak of lightning and slip without a scratch down a honey locust; can whip my weight in wild cats,—and if any gentleman pleases, for a ten dollar bill, he may throw in a panther . . .

This speech, and variations on it, have been attributed to Crockett from that time to this. He probably never actually said it (although we shouldn't put it past Crockett to adapt the colorful speech for himself), but it's pure Nimrod Wildfire.

From the author's collection.

Later, David Crockett acknowledged his connection to Paulding's play a bit more directly. In 1833, James Hackett returned to the United States after a highly successful European tour. By now, he was not performing *The Lion of the West* in its entirety; instead, he staged a kind of "greatest hits" show of all of his most famous characters. He was to give this performance in Washington, and Congressman Crockett himself reserved a box seat. When Hackett strode out on stage in the character of Colonel Nimrod Wildfire, resplendent in buckskin and fur hat (still wildcat, not raccoon-skin), he paused for a moment and looked upward at Crockett. Smiling, Hackett bowed deeply. Crockett stood and bowed back, to the delighted cheers of the audience. In that moment, as Crockett scholar Paul Andrew Hutton has written, "reality and legend melded for a cosmic moment into one."[11]

Frank Hitchcock Murdock and Frank Mayo's popular *Davy Crockett, Or, Be Sure You're Right, Then Go Ahead* yielded no such cosmic moments, even though Susannah Dickinson/Hannig attended a performance. But this play actually connects more meaningfully to the enduring Crockett legend than does Paulding's crude Colonel Wildfire.

The play, of course, had very little to do with the real Davy Crockett; it didn't even pretend to. It was based loosely on the story of Lochinvar, the hero of a Sir Walter Scott poem who steals away his love just as she is about to be married to another. The play depicts the 25-year-old Davy Crockett as a barely literate mountain man and hunter who is also handsome, good-hearted, highly principled, and tirelessly brave. The climax of the play comes when wolves attack Davy's cabin. Having used the cabin beam for firewood, Davy has to protect his lover all night long by barring the door with his arm. In the third act we find him still barring the door with his swollen arm; and he says, rather ingenuously, "This is getting kind of monotonous, this business is." Scholars have since argued whether the humor of the line is intentional. But a reading of the play reveals a great deal of endearing—if a bit obvious—rural comedy, and this deadpan line is entirely in keeping with the tone of the play and its humor.

Like Lochinvar, Davy is at first prepared to give up his ladylove to the rich, powerful man to whom she is engaged. But on her wedding day, Davy appears on horseback and spirits her away. The gesture is both heroic and romantic, everything we expect of legendary Davy.

Paulding's Nimrod Wildfire is more closely linked to the buffoonish, sometimes revolting Crockett of the famous "Crockett Almanacs." About forty-five Crockett Almanacs were published between 1835 and 1856. Like any farmer's almanac, these little booklets were filled with farming hints, aphorisms, cartoons, and stories. The tales about Crockett emphasized his crude, rather obnoxious sense of humor and introduced many of the tall tales that have become a permanent part of the Crockett legend. That image has nearly been washed from the pub-

THE ALAMO

In Memory of the Fallen Heroes of Texas.

Words by

Mrs. Jennie Myers.

PATRIOTIC SONG
and
CHORUS.

Music by

Miss Ella Rodeffer.

🌟

✺ 4 ✺

🌟

PUBLISHED BY

J. MYERS and E. RODEFFER,

SAN ANTONIO, TEXAS.

Northrop, Nagel & Jent, Print., San Antonio, Texas.

From the author's collection.

"HOWL AWAY. YOU'LL HAVE TO SCATTER BEFORE DAWN."

A rare poster advertising Frank Hitchcock Murdock's long-running play, *Davy Crockett: Or, Be Sure You're Right, Then Go Ahead,* starring Frank Mayo. This poster depicts the climax of the play, when Davy bars the door with his arm against savage wolves. From the collection of Paul Andrew Hutton.

lic consciousness by more than a century of image cleansing, courtesy of John Wayne, Fess Parker—and Frank Mayo.

The theater has proven more amenable to comedies and melodramas about Davy Crockett than about his final struggle at the Alamo. Part of this has to do with simple logistics: To properly convey the battle of the Alamo on stage, a large cast is necessary, as well as imposing sets and noisy stagecraft. Even if done well, an Alamo play is unlikely to fully engage an audience. The story is simply too complex, too epic, too reliant on the climactic battle.

However, several ambitious playwrights have given it the old college try. In fact, one anonymous Johnny-on-the-spot got right to work, apparently as soon as he heard the tragic news from Texas. The June 2, 1836, edition of the *Boston Morning Post* reported this intriguing item:

> *The Fall of Alamo,* dramatised, has been brought out at the
> Arch Street Theatre, Philadelphia. Mr. Walton personates
> Colonel Travis. Mr. Hathwell Colonel Crockett, and Mr. Darley
> does Santa Anna. It must be a bloody affair.

Unfortunately, we don't currently know much else about this production. However, taking into consideration how slowly news traveled at the time, a June dramatization of an event that had happened less than three months earlier is astonishing in itself. *The Fall of Alamo* was subtitled *Texas and the Oppressors.* The Arch Street Theatre company followed the production less than a week later with a benefit performance of *Othello.* "The curtain descended somewhat incongruously with the cast singing, 'All for Texas, or Volunteers for Glory.'"[12]

The next Alamo drama didn't come along until over forty years later. Francis Nona's *The Fall of the Alamo,* an almost impenetrable exercise in turgid theatrics, first bored audiences in 1879. In 1886, Hiram H. McLane produced a similarly unpromising piece—a play *in blank verse* that droned on for four interminable acts, including prologue. At least his heart was in the right place. The San Antonio author wrote in the preface to the published version of his play that he intended for the work to raise money for "a suitable MONUMENT on the spot where they fell, to that band of noble men who sacrificed their lives for their country."[13]

To give his play some background, McLane published excerpts from Henderson K. Yoakum's *History of Texas* as an appendix—which is just as well, since otherwise the reader or viewer would often find himself at sea. This is particularly true because McLane found it necessary to write all of his dialogue in nearly indecipherable dialect. At the end, Crockett finds himself the last man standing. A Mexican officer approaches to ask him to surrender. Crockett, thinking that the man wants to fight, politely lays down his own weapon, since his enemy doesn't seem to have one. And these are his last words (and McLane's final stage direction):

> Thar, flank 'round thar, little ones,
> And let me pitch inter him

Like a thousand o' brick:
I'll show an old blab-mouthed blatherskite
    like him
How ter come 'round har
And tuk up uther folks' fites, I will.
Whoopee, thar! Look out thar, old coon,
I'm a cummin', I ar!
And now squar yerself
Fer kerzip, I'll tuk yer!

[*He spits on his hands, and leaps over the bodies around him, in the direction of Santa Anna, when he is knocked down by the soldiers, and bayoneted.*]

THE END

Now, is that any way for a former congressman to talk? And is that any way for a play to end?

In 1935, Franklin Y. Martin came up with a much more palatable and, mercifully, shorter little play called *Death Comes to the Alamo*. Martin intended the play for amateur or school groups, suggesting that slapsticks could be used for gunfire. He wrote in the foreword that he wanted the play to "present historical facts in an entertaining form" but also stressed that his "higher ideal in these pages is to stimulate patriotism in the public schools and, at the same time, subdue racial prejudice."[14]

Because the story of the Alamo has sometimes been a flashpoint for Anglo-Hispanic bitterness, Martin's aims for his play were admirable. They were, however, a tad heavy-handed. One of his characters, a young Alamo defender named Flanders, speaks frequently and passionately about his hatred of Mexicans. In the final battle, he and a Mexican soldier fire simultaneously, mortally wounding each other. The nearness of death seems to cure Flanders of his racism.

FLANDERS [*raising himself weakly, leaning on an elbow and speaking to the Mexican*]: Well, you got me 'Meck.' [*holding hand over heart*] Close to the heart. [*smiling and speaking in jest*] Congratulations. It was a dandy shot.
MEXICAN: Me die, too.

Hobart Bosworth was one of the screen's first Crocketts. His 1910 film, *Davy Crockett*, was an adaptation of the Murdock/Mayo play. Courtesy of Marc Wanamaker and Bison Archives.

FLANDERS: And I reckon—it's nobody's fault—I see a light there, see? [*pointing up*] A great light—in the shape of a cross— and it's coming this way. I see men, and they're wounded— there's One with a wound in His side. [*emotionally*] It's Christ— and there's Travis with Him; and Crockett—and—there's the Mexican I killed on the wall. How beautiful he looks in the light of Christ. [*pause*] I feel rested, and happy; and it's funny—I don't hate—anybody—any more.

You have to admit, that's a heck of a final breath. And, despite Martin's ambitions for his work, it can't escape the reader's notice that, while the playwright gives Flanders plenty of high-flown ideas about forgiveness and racial prejudice, he gives the only Mexican in the play a single line: "Me die, too." However, any true Alamo-worshipping Texan should find the scene inordinately satisfying in one sense at least. For once, Travis and Crockett are right there with Jesus where they belong. Unfortunately, Bowie dies after Flanders, so the audience is left hanging regarding his place in paradise.

Despite the over-the-top quality of Flanders's demise, *Death Comes to the Alamo* is a surprisingly thoughtful little play, particularly since it was aimed at younger performers and audiences. The language is a bit flowery and the characters of Bowie, Travis, and Crockett are even more pure and flawless than they usually are, but Martin creates some very nice moments in his very traditional Alamo:

CROCKETT: This pile of masonry doesn't make the church, anyway. The most hallowed church I was ever in was an unin- habited valley I wandered into—up in the Cumberlands. And every stone and tree testified to the presence of God.

FLANDERS [*jestingly*]: I'm glad this *is* a church. It will be sort of comforting at Judgement to know you died in a church.

STOCKTON: Please—don't talk that way. It makes me shudder to hear one jesting in the presence of death. This is no time for nonsense.

And later . . .

FLANDERS: I hear their bands playing. I guess they've already started celebrating their victory.

TRAVIS: They're playing the "Cut-throat." We can expect no quarter.

CROCKETT: And we're asking for none.

The following year, 1936, was the Texas Centennial, an event that saw countless celebrations all over the state. Many of them included dramas or outdoor pageants or other theatrical treatments of Texas's historical past. One major work was *Tejas: A Dramatic Opera in Three Acts Commemorating the 100th Anniversary of Texas* with a libretto by May Abney Mayes and Willie Megee McGhee and music by Theosophus Fitz. Before the opera was performed in its entirety at San Antonio's Municipal Auditorium, a select audience heard a preview within the walls of the Alamo itself. On the evening of March 5, 1936, the centenary of the eve of the Alamo's fall, baritone Rufus Craddox and contralto Monette Shaw performed "The Deadline," a musical rendition of Travis's drawing of the line.

Craddock played Travis and Mrs. Shaw played Susannah Dickinson. In addition to giving over the Alamo to this performance, the DRT also allowed Mr. Craddock to use "a real Alamo relic" as his sword. The performance was also broadcast over WOAI radio at 10:30 p.m. and was introduced by San Antonio's Mayor C. K. Quin, who said:

> We stand with bowed heads in our historic shrine which, in
> the early hours of morning ran red with martyr blood. Let us all
> resolve anew, as did the heroes of Texas and twenty other states,
> to stand for the right against the wrong and thus be worthy of
> the heritage they vouchsafed to us.[15]

Regardless of the musical and dramatic merits of *Tejas,* the scene performed that night did offer a version of the famous line scene that was unlike any other:

COL. TRAVIS
Our food is fast dwindling, my men;
Our ammunition is low.
Santa Anna has ten times as many;
Shall we remain or shall we go?

Alamo dramas have been both great and small. This play, "Remember the Alamo," was performed in 1971 by the sixth-grade class of Cuba Private School, Cuba, Alabama. Their teacher, who also wrote and directed the play, was Joan Headley. An Alamo enthusiast, she later went on to spearhead the restoration of the William Barret Travis home in Clairborne, Alabama. Photographs by Joan Headley.

Shall we fail to fire the signal gun
At the rising of tomorrow's sun?

Would that Houston or Fannin might come
To relieve our distress ere we die.
There is yet time to escape,
Or shall we their hordes defy?
Remember the Spartans at Thermopylae,
Were they braver men than we?

Come over the line and stand with me,
To die like brave men we.
We will build the altar higher
For the sacrifice and slaughter
And when our bodies are wrapped in smoke
From our funeral pyre.

May some loyal kind Texan turn
Toward the burning bier
And may the sight no sigh evoke

As he cools our ashes with a tear
Let him take our ashes from the dust
And place them in a silver urn;
Graven let its motto be
In God we trust.

Ramsey Yelvington's 1954 drama of the Alamo, *A Cloud of Witnesses,* also allowed William Barret Travis a poetic speech at his moment of decision. But unlike the Travis of *Tejas,* Yelvington's commander is consumed less with the poignancy of sacrifice than with a fatalistic, almost religious, sense of duty:

See this sword?
A drawn sword!

Unsheathed, naked,
To be clothed in blood!

Look at it!
Look at it long!
You are this blade
And God made you strong!

Who will follow me?
Follow the sword?
Follow the sword
Of our precious Lord!
Here I draw a blood-red line
For you to cross
Or stay behind.
Who will be first to follow me,
To throw down his life
For Liberty?

And where *Tejas*—as well as most dramatic depictions of Travis's drawing of the line—takes the incident as an inspiring fact, Yelvington has other aims. One of the members of the garrison, Moses Rose, does not cross the line. In fact, in *A Cloud of Witnesses,* Rose is also Satan, which is perhaps a bit harsher than the old Frenchman deserves. Still, Rose/Satan explains to the audience, and his "cloud of witnesses," why he stayed put, instead of stepping across the line with the other martyrs:

Satan: And now may I have just a moment to explain why I didn't cross over the line? Because, like all myths and legends that spring up without corroboration from the most unlikely situations, this scene never happened. It's rank fiction. It's pure myth. There never was any line to cross over!

The widows of the Gonzales men who died in the Alamo act as a kind of Greek chorus for the play. They are outraged and rebuke Satan in unison:

Oh, is that so?
Well, we know you,
And even if what you said were true,
We know our men

And we say, true or untrue,
It would have been just like them!

With this response, Yelvington steps firmly into the ranks of what we might call the clear-eyed Alamo traditionalist—the historian or enthusiast who accepts that many of the Alamo myths are not literally true, but feels that by embracing them, we can find a deeper truth in the event. If that smacks more of religion than history, so be it; the Alamo itself crossed that line many, many years ago.

Ramsey Yelvington's *A Cloud of Witnesses* was first presented at Baylor University in 1954 during the annual Conference of American Ideals. Yelvington, never having been able to attend any of the rehearsals, saw his play for the first time with an audience that, to all appearances, didn't like it at all. Director Paul Baker wrote:

> The play was performed, and the audience arose hot and sticky from their seats in complete silence and filed out into the sunlit lobby, saying almost nothing. Mr. Yelvington afterward admitted that he thought the whole thing had been a complete bust. Happily, he was wrong, the audience had in fact been both moved and amazed, and gave evidence of their approval when he was introduced that evening at the formal banquet.[16]

For such a difficult play—it is written in blank verse and is more concerned with psychological and spiritual matters more than historical ones—*A Cloud of Witnesses* has been surprisingly popular over the years, revived regularly and reviewed enthusiastically. Its second production was mounted in July 1955 on the grounds of San Antonio's beautiful Mission San Jose, where according to its director, Paul Baker, the play seemed to have been granted heavenly approval:

> A huge Texas moon slowly rose through the feathery huisache and retama trees behind the rugged skeletal set, and, as though by arrangement, hovered above the peak of the familiar Alamo façade just at the climax of the play; then it rose distantly in the heavens as the smoke from the burning pyres of bodies signaled the sad conclusion. It was a night to be cherished through a lifetime by all lovers of real theater.[17]

The title of *A Cloud of Witnesses* comes from the Bible. In Hebrews 12:1–2, St. Paul wrote that all the souls in Heaven observe the actions of the living on Earth.

> Wherefore, seeing we also are compassed about with so great a cloud of witnesses, let us lay aside every weight, and the sin which doth so easily best us, and let us run with patience the race that is set before us, looking unto Jesus the author and finisher of our faith; who for the joy that was set before him endured the cross, despising the shame, and is set down at the right hand of the throne of God.

In the play, the "cloud of witnesses" are the Alamo dead and the Gonzales women who have gathered in the modern-day Alamo to remind the living of their sacrifice. They are met there by Satan who, like an evil therapist, leads them through a voyage of self-discovery. His question, which the other characters spend the play trying to answer, is, "Hasn't Freedom changed?"

TEXANS
We thought we felt the evil presence. Satan!

WOMEN
Of course!
Isn't he said to be myth? Isn't he legend?
Yet you are free and he tempted you—

TEXANS
With a question!

WOMEN
Yes!
Can he by one simple question so easily confuse you?
Do you not remember the place, the time?
Do you forget so soon?

The set constructed for Ramsey Yelvington's drama of the Alamo, *A Cloud of Witnesses*. Courtesy of *LIFE Magazine*.

TEXANS
> We remember.
> We remember the cold, the hunger, the hurt;
> We remember the crying for sleep, the pain.

WOMEN
> But do you remember the condition?
> Do you remember the cause, the reason why?

TEXANS
> We remember. We recall:
> The siege. The fall.
> And the reason why.
> It was for Freedom that we died.

The "cloud of witnesses." From the author's collection.

And the condition *is* the same—Freedom has not changed!
Our dying kept it living, kept it safe,
And from our dust, the mammoth thing, Freedom,
Received a forward thrust
That has continually reverberated.

A Cloud of Witnesses is one of the most compelling and convincing Alamo dramatizations *because* of its stylization, its artificiality. The characters rarely speak in conversational English, and the settings and characterizations are abstract and poetic, but Yelvington gets at the dramatic truths of the Alamo—at least, the mythic, inspirational Alamo—better than any other playwright or filmmaker.

Ramsey Yelvington saw the battle of the Alamo in terms of heroism and sacrifice, principles and loss, love and death. But he didn't make much of the racial or cultural aspects of the event. The Tejano defend-

Crockett, Bowie, and Travis from *A Cloud of Witnesses*. From the author's collection.

ers and their wives and children are present but not prominent in *A Cloud of Witnesses*. Neither is the Mexican army depicted in villainous terms. For Yelvington, Moses Rose the coward, not Santa Anna the enemy, represents the horror of the Alamo. It is Rose who has tinged the otherwise flawless sacrifice of the Alamo garrison, and Rose (and Satan) who must be rebuked by their ghosts.

But few subsequent theatrical treatments of the battle of the Alamo would be able to avoid its racial aspects. Playwright Sandra de Helen constructed her one-act play, *My Alamo* (1999), around the dilemma of Captain Juan Nepomuceno Seguin, who urges Travis to fall back in order to fight Santa Anna more effectively elsewhere. Both Travis and Crockett regard Seguin with suspicion, because they believe that as a Tejano, Seguin's sympathies lie more with Mexico than Texas. They also suspect he is a coward.

De Helen depicts Travis as stubborn and shortsighted, insisting that the men of the Alamo have an excellent chance of winning the upcoming fight or at least holding out until help arrives. She depicts Crockett as, predictably enough, a folksy yarn-spinner and, somewhat less predictably, as "slightly effeminate." This characterization apparently comes from the questionable testimony of Madame Candelaria, a Mexican woman who, in her old age, used to sit before the Alamo telling tales to tourists. She claimed to have nursed Jim Bowie through the siege, but there is no evidence that she was in the Alamo at all. In a newspaper interview in the *San Antonio Light* (February 19, 1899), she described Crockett in this way:

> He was the strangest man I ever saw. He had the face of a woman, and his manner that of a girl. I could never regard him as a hero until I saw him die. He looked grand and terrible, standing at the front door and fighting a whole column of Mexican infantry.

In Sandra de Helen's *My Alamo,* the only people Crockett fights are Travis, Bowie, and Seguin. In her synopsis of the play, de Helen writes:

> All hell breaks loose when Bowie accuses Crockett of being "pansy-assed" and Travis of being biased against Hispanics, specifically Bowie's own wife. Finally, when it becomes clear that

Seguin's council won't be taken, Seguin volunteers to leave the Alamo, certain he is facing death, to go for help. Instead, of course, it is the others who die at the hands of Santa Anna's army when no one arrives to save them.[18]

Bernard J. Taylor's musical, *Liberty! The Siege of the Alamo* (1999), also deals with ethnic struggles within the Alamo and without. Jim Bowie sings "Torn Between Two Cultures" about being an Anglo with a Mexican wife. And Juan Seguin explains his position in "I Am a Tejano," in which he asserts that Texas is his home and that he "owes no allegiance to Spain or Mexico." But Taylor wanted to accomplish more than an examination of racial strife at the Alamo; he wanted to celebrate the event, which he sees in purely heroic terms. Taylor told a reporter:

> What annoys me is that there are people here trying to dis-
> credit the defenders. Crockett, for instance. They try to diminish
> him by saying he surrendered and was executed. He was a brave
> man. You can't get away from that.[19]

Taylor, a British playwright, wrote his musical as a response to the cynicism of the times. "What happened at the Alamo," he said, "is the essence of what America stands for. America is the bedrock of individual liberty."[20] Taylor claimed to have done considerable research on the Alamo, but was careful to craft his production around inspirational themes of valor and traditional acceptance of the Alamo myth, which, according to Alamo curator Bruce Winders, is a perfectly acceptable approach. Winders told a reporter that Taylor had consulted with him on a few matters. "I talked to him about some of the recent controversies surrounding the Alamo," Winders said. "But art is art and history is history, so if people want accuracy in every historic detail, there are better sources to find them than in art."[21]

Taylor's cast of Alamo characters is constructed entirely upon the normal party line (all cast members named here are from the original San Antonio production): Bowie (Richard Warren) and Travis (Tom Miller) are at each other's throats, but resolve their differences when Bowie becomes ill. Crockett (Michael Lee Berlet) is in Texas searching for a new beginning. Although perceived as a legend, he sings, he is "just a man, doing the best he can." Santa Anna (Rene Sandoval) is a vicious tyrant; and the Dickinsons (Jesse Pottebaum and Becky King) are an optimistic young couple whose happiness is cut short by his sense of duty. Taylor also brings in a laundry list of Alamo defenders—John McGregor, Charles Zanco, Micajah Autry, and others—who enter, sing little songs to introduce themselves, and then go away.

Oddly, Taylor chose to make Travis's slave Joe (Rufus Jackson) an old man instead of the 23-year-old he actually was. One wonders if he wasn't influenced more by the fictional slave Jethro (Jester Hairston) in John Wayne's *The Alamo* than by any historical description of the real Joe. Worse, Taylor gave Joe some awkward and uncomfortable "Amos 'n' Andy"-style dialogue. Even worse yet, the playwright placed Joe in one of the most embarrassing scenes in recent theater. Travis good-naturedly explains to Joe why his slavery is all in his head, and that he has choices to make, just like any man. The scene and the song "Freedom," which accompanies it, can be described at best as being in atrociously bad taste, and at worst as truly flesh-crawlingly offensive.

Otherwise, Taylor didn't take many liberties with what we know about these characters, nor with the story of the siege itself, which doggedly progresses from point A to point B without a single surprising perspective. The final battle is handled expressionistically, with flashes of light, a montage of battle sounds and scraps of songs, and a series of slides depicting Alamo artwork.

Liberty! The Siege of the Alamo had its world premiere at the Josephine Theatre in San Antonio on November 11, 1999. Directed by Missy Miller, the cast of thirty performed to a prerecorded musical that utilized synthesizers instead of genuine orchestral instruments. Unfortunately, the cast recording of the score that has been released on compact disc uses the same track. It lends a distinctly amateurish sound to the entire enterprise and, worse, often makes the production come off like a "Saturday Night Live"-style parody of a musical. However, the local press treated the premiere rather kindly. *Express-News* arts writer, Deborah Martin, wrote of the show's "compelling moments" and "hummable music," but did not neglect its "hokey moments":

"A significant low point is 'Freedom,'" she wrote, "a chipper little song about personal choice and freedom that, in an unseemly move, Travis sings to his slave." Martin also pointed out that "there's not much character development in the piece. And the already thin sketches of the characters are reduced even more by some fairly weak performances. Several characters come off as caricatures."[22]

Perhaps Taylor's most serious misstep was the understandable one of overambition. In trying to address all aspects of the siege and pay homage to many of the participants on either side, both famous and obscure, he simply bit off more than he could chew. He was trying to deal with too many characters and too many ideas. In the process, he traded in depth and characterization for what he perceived as the Big Picture.

Actor-playwright Jerry Strickler took precisely the opposite approach. In his one-man play *My Alamo Family,* Strickler told the story of the siege and fall of the Alamo through the eyes of a single character, Robert Allen, using no props and a bare set. With shades of Ramsey Yelvington's *A Cloud of Witnesses,* Strickler's character is a ghost who has come back to make sense of what he went through in his short life. When Strickler performed the show in Scotland, a local critic wrote that the actor's

> talent and personality come across like a prairie fire, so it all
> comes vividly to life . . . he recreates the siege and the life before-
> hand: the scouting, the buffalo hunt, settlers against injuns,
> Bowie's knife-fighting, Crockett's shooting, the music, the loving
> and above all, the hopeless last stand. The sweep of the West
> comes to life, bold and bloody, black and bawdy, the whole
> delivered with deep feeling and not a few laughs.[23]

Perhaps Strickler found the key to dramatizing the Alamo story on stage. Where others have crowded the stage with actors and tried to concoct stage effects that would simulate the fury of battle, Strickler boiled the story down to its essence—a tale of sacrifice, yes. But more important, a tale of ordinary people and how they made their way through an extraordinary time.

CHAPTER ★6★

The Cinematic Alamo

Among the audiences who saw the very first motion picture about the battle of the Alamo were people who were old enough to remember the actual event. *The Immortal Alamo,* a one-reel treatment of the subject, was filmed on location in San Antonio. It was released in May 1911, only seventy-five years after the Alamo's siege and fall.

More intriguingly, there were people living in San Antonio at the time that the film was produced who had actually participated in the battle of the Alamo. We don't know if any of them had the curiosity—or, perhaps, the stomach—to attend one of the nickelodeon showings of *The Immortal Alamo,* but their mere proximity is fascinating. We tend to think of the battle of the Alamo as a rather remote historic event and the invention of the moving picture camera as relatively modern. It seems slightly disorienting that both events could actually have occurred within a single lifetime.

If any participants in the Alamo tragedy actually did see *The Immortal Alamo,* they must have been nonplussed, if not absolutely mystified. For, like virtually every film and television production about the Alamo, it was a fiction dressed up with sprinkles of fact. In the previous century novelists, poets, and playwrights had played fast and loose with the history of the Alamo; but when filmmakers got hold of the subject, their embroidery of fantasy wasn't so easily dismissed as a mere story. The films were imbued with a sense of dimension that made them seem more immediate, more genuine, more true.

The movies, for better or worse, have had an enormous effect on the study of the Alamo—and on our perception of what happened there,

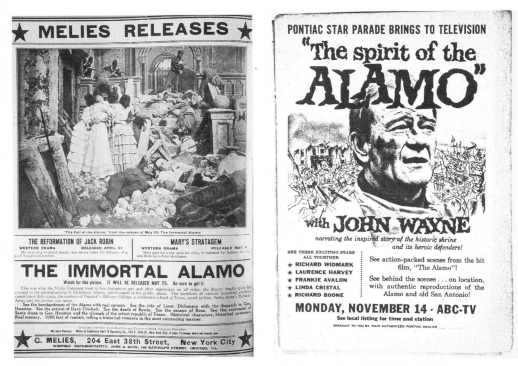

Left: The first Alamo movie—*The Immortal Alamo,* released in May 1911. From the author's collection.

Right: The premiere of John Wayne's *The Alamo* was soon followed by a one-hour television special, videotaped on the set in 1959. "The Spirit of the Alamo" aired on November 14, 1960. From the collection of Craig R. Covner.

and why. Nearly every current serious historian of the subject caught the Alamo bug from Fess Parker or John Wayne and from the accompanying comic books, toys, and other ephemera. The best of these historians are able to separate history from pop culture; but those images are sometimes indelible, and even the best intentions can't quite dispel them.

The trouble is that the filmmakers who produce all the Alamo movies have always sung the same song of authenticity. They all claim complete and utter fidelity to fact. But facts rarely creep into any Alamo movie. If we watch them to learn history, we are only deluding ourselves. But if we enjoy them in the right spirit—that is, as fanciful and entertaining celebrations of the Alamo myth—the Alamo movies can not only be great fun, but they can actually add to our understanding of what the

From the collection of Paul Andrew Hutton.

Alamo means. However, they rarely add much to our understanding of what actually happened in February and March of 1836.

Sometimes the movies steer us wrong in ways we don't immediately perceive. As adults, few of us would watch Disney's *Davy Crockett, King of the Wild Frontier* (1955) with any delusion that it presents an accurate picture of the time or place. We know that there was not really a Bustedluck or a Thimblerig or a Georgie Russel. But watching, as children, the final image—of Davy at the top of those stairs, whacking Mexicans over the head with his rifle-club—seemed to seep into some secret part of our minds. We know it didn't happen that way, but it seems so right somehow.

Although that image is firmly implanted in our imaginations, it might later inspire us to seek out the truth of what really happened to Davy—even if we don't want to believe it. In this case, the inaccurate film has actually stimulated us to learn more, to get closer to history.

But other Alamo images aren't so easily dispelled.

In the introduction to this book, I wrote about my first visit to the set of John Wayne's *The Alamo* when I was eleven. The ruined set at Alamo Village seemed so much more authentic to me than the real Alamo did. And for years, it served as a kind of reference point to me about what the Alamo "really" looked like—I knew, because I had actually been there.

Lieutenant Dickinson (William Carroll) and his wife "Lucy" (Edith Storey) enjoy an idyllic moment in *The Immortal Alamo* (1911), unaware that trouble is lurking in the person of Señor Navarre (Francis Ford; second from right). Courtesy Academy of Motion Picture Arts and Sciences.

In fact, as constructed for and used in the film, the set was reasonably convincing; but hardly authentic. Its problems are small, in some ways, but significant. First, the mission compound was built at only three-quarters of the original scale. The Alamo church was full size, but represented a kind of hodgepodge of inspirations, mixing the ruined elements of the genuine 1836 Alamo with the anachronistic upper windows that were added years after the battle. Less noticeable are the columns bordering the icon niches; their spirals go the wrong way. And only the façade of the church is constructed from limestone—the rest of the building is adobe. Wayne and his art director, Al Ybarra, built their Alamo on the ranch of James T. "Happy" Shahan. It's a picturesque place, but doesn't much resemble the land around the Alamo in 1836. Wayne's Alamo sits alone on a barren plain, nothing like the lush river shorelines of the real San Antonio of those days. In perhaps the most significant deviation from fact, the town of San Antonio is due south of the mission instead of west across the river (and, of course, there's no river).

Heroes of the Alamo (1937) is the only Alamo film in which the Dickinsons, Almeron (Bruce Warren) and Susannah (Ruth Findlay), serve as the main characters. From the collection of Paul Andrew Hutton.

Obviously, these niggling details can't steer us *too* wrong. Or can they?

Well, yes they can. The smaller scale of the mission compound tends to make Wayne's Alamo seem far more populated than it should be. We are told constantly that the Alamo is defended by "a small band of soldiers," but there always seems to be plenty of them, all over the place. There is no earthen ramp leading up to the apse of the church where the cannon crew should be. In fact, the church seems to be included for purely cosmetic reasons only; not much goes on in there. Because there is neither a river nor any of the other buildings that were really outside the Alamo's walls, the movie battle takes on an entirely different character from the actual struggle in 1836 (setting aside, of course, the fact that it's fought in broad daylight instead of in the predawn hours).

The irony is that with all the blatant inaccuracies of Wayne's film—and let us not mince words here: *The Alamo* is a *total* work of fiction, unmarked by a single authentic moment, word, detail, costume, or action—the set looks pretty good. It's at least *reasonably* authentic, and that's more than you can say for the set of virtually any other Alamo film before or since. It's so close to being authentic, in fact, that it seeps into our subconscious a little deeper than it otherwise might. It gets easier and easier to picture that set in our mind's eye while reading Walter Lord. Even many modern-day artists paint battle scenes, crowing about their in-depth research, when they have clearly used the ever more inaccurate Wayne set as their model.

Most Alamo films don't present us with that problem. Most of them are so far off the mark that we never really fool ourselves into thinking that we're looking at an accurate picture of the place or the time. As history, nearly every Alamo film is worthless; but only a fool would try to learn history from a movie, anyway. What films *can* do is to offer their viewers a doorway to historic events. Dramatic movies aren't as much about learning as they are about feeling; they offer celebration, not explanation. Even at their most simplistic, Alamo films offer their own kind of truth that doesn't have anything to do with fact—an image here, a word there, moments of understanding, of emotional clarity.

That is why my discussion of what is and isn't authentic in Alamo movies ends here. Most of them don't even try, although nearly all of them claim to. But each one has enormous value on its own terms; each is a portrait not of the historical Alamo but of the Alamo as seen in different periods and from widely divergent points of view.

Perhaps the best way to look at this is to consider how each of the main characters has been presented in film after film, for it is through them that the filmmakers attempt to speak directly to their audience. Deciding whether Santa Anna will be a buffoon, a wise leader, a snarling devil, or an egocentric tyrant is how each filmmaker hones their point of view and chooses at which cultural target to aim their particular Alamo.

The first Alamo film may have bitten off a bit more than it could chew. In this single reel—which would run about fifteen minutes, more or less—*The Immortal Alamo* (1911) presents a love story, the saga of the Alamo, *and* a depiction of the battle of San Jacinto. In doing so, it tosses history to the four winds, allowing one of the prominent Alamo martyrs not only to survive the battle but to lead Sam Houston's army on its vengeful ride, like the cavalry in a B-Western.

Susannah (Virginia Grey) and Almeron (John Russell) bid each other farewell inside the Alamo church—built on a soundstage at Republic Pictures in Hollywood—in *The Last Command* (1955). Courtesy of Republic Pictures.

The Dickinsons

While *The Immortal Alamo* might have been simple—perhaps even simplistic—it is one of the very few films to concentrate on the Dickinsons, as opposed to the big three of Crockett, Bowie, and Travis. In fact, there are no surviving stills to suggest that Crockett and Bowie are even *in* this film. In *Immortal Alamo,* the Dickinsons' story is almost totally fictionalized. Her name is Lucy, not Susannah. They have no child. She is kidnapped at the Alamo and nearly forced into marriage with a villainous Mexican. And Lt. Dickinson rides in with Houston to dispatch the bad guy. But authentic or not, the fact that the Dickinsons are central to the film is nearly unique.

Anthony Xydias's *Heroes of the Alamo* (1937, directed by Harry Fraser) is the only other film that places the Dickinsons at the heart of the story. Al and Anne, the "Dickinson" couple portrayed by Bruce Warren and Ruth Findlay, represent the Texas of the future—hard-working pioneers who dream of Texas's potential. On the eve of the battle, Anne says passionately to Al, "Whatever happens to us, Texas will go on. A Texas so great, so wonderful in the years to come that you and I can't even imagine it. But without us, without the Alamo, that Texas could never be. Why, its life will be our lives."

Few of the Alamo's characters are presented in such diverse ways as Susannah Dickinson. While her presence didn't seem to have much impact one way or the other on the historical Alamo, she is invaluable to the Alamo myth as mother, widow, survivor, and woman. There were, of course, several women and children in the fort during the siege. And though nearly all of them walked out of the Alamo on the morning of March 6, 1836, only Susannah and her daughter Angelina kept walking right into legend. In *The Immortal Alamo,* "Lucy" Dickinson's role (played by Edith Storey) is primarily a sexual one. She is a newlywed and has no child. When her husband is sent as a courier to fetch Houston to come to the aid of the Alamo, Lucy is left at the mercy of the treacherous Mexican spy, Navarre (Francis Ford). Thus it is that when Houston's forces come riding down on Santa Anna at the end of the film, they are not only avenging the Alamo massacre but also preventing the "forced marriage" (read: rape) between Lucy and Navarre.

The Susannah Dickinson of W. Christy Cabanne's *The Martyrs of the Alamo or The Birth of Texas* (1915) also has to fend off unwelcome advances from amorous Mexicans. *Martyrs of the Alamo* was supervised (produced) by D. W. Griffith and is cut from the same racist cloth as *Birth of a Nation,* Griffith's masterpiece of the same year. Like the "arrogant" Reconstruction-era Blacks of *Birth of a Nation,* the Mexicans of *Martyrs of the Alamo* are damned in the filmmakers' eyes not for their political threat but for their disrespect of White men and

---

John Wayne didn't mess with the legend—in his *Alamo,* Mrs. Dickinson (Joan O'Brien) and daughter Angelina (Aissa Wayne) are the only Anglo survivors. They are accompanied not by Travis's slave, Joe (who doesn't appear in the film), but by a fictional child named in the credits (but not in the film) as "Happy Sam," played by John Henry Daniels. Courtesy of Batjac Prod.

Almeron Dickinson (Fred Burns) fights to the death in *Martyrs of the Alamo* (1915). From the author's collection.

their mindless lust for White women. While Susannah (Ora Carew) makes her way home through streets crowded with drunken, rowdy Mexican soldiers, a suave officer begins to flirt with her. She angrily rebuffs his advances and goes home. When her husband Almeron (Fred Burns) learns of this offense, he goes right out and shoots the officer dead. Cabanne and Griffith clearly support this action; they present the shooting as entirely deserved. Dickinson is arrested for it—and *he* looks like the victim! His jailing becomes the rallying point for other Americans who have also, we are told, been living under these intolerable conditions.

Unlike "Lucy" from *Immortal Alamo,* the Susannah of *Martyrs of the Alamo* is a mother, but her child is never given any kind of personality; it's just a baby in a blanket. At the end of the film, Susannah's loss is not the rupture of her family but the loss of her husband's romantic attention. She watches sadly as two survivors of the Alamo embrace and dream of a future together. She walks away (with no baby in sight) as a title tells us that the broken-hearted woman "could not forget at what price came victory."

But Ruth Findlay's Anne Dickinson from *Heroes of the Alamo* (1937) is both wife and mother. Left at home while Al (Bruce Warren) is off revolutionizing with his pals, Anne feels that she should be by his side, helping him. When her daughter says, "I want my daddy. I want my daddy right now!" Anne decides to "run the gauntlet" and enter the

Alamo. Though a couple of Mexican soldiers shoot at her with rifles apparently equipped with whistles (you'll have to hear it to believe it), she bangs on the Alamo gate and is let inside. Confronted by Travis, Anne says defiantly, "I'm a Texas woman. I couldn't just sit at home. I'll nurse the men. I'll do anything. But I won't leave!" Once in the Alamo, the lives of Anne and Angelina are in danger, but this matters less to them than the fact that the family is whole once again. In putting the Dickinsons at the forefront of the film, *Heroes of the Alamo* suggests that Texas will survive not merely through the sacrifice of the men of the Alamo, but because the burdens and rewards are shared by all—it's the most democratic of Alamo films. (It is worth mentioning that the low-budget *Heroes of the Alamo* was padded with battle footage from an earlier Anthony J. Xydias release, *With Davy Crockett at the Fall of the Alamo* (1926), starring Cullin Landis. Significantly, the Dickinsons don't show up in this silent film at all; it is strictly the story of Crockett, Bowie, and Travis.)

The Susannah Dickinson of the movies is a character in constant transition. She weeps and cowers in *Martyrs of the Alamo*; swoons as her husband avenges her in *The Immortal Alamo*, and stands stoically by with her baby daughter as both her husband and son are killed together in *The Alamo: Shrine of Texas Liberty* (1938).

The Dickinsons, for some reason, have been awarded an extra child in *Shrine of Texas Liberty* and in *The Last Command* (1955). It isn't quite clear why the screenwriters came up with a son for the Dickinsons, but the roots of their decision might come from a persistent Alamo myth. It was said that during the battle, one of the defenders placed a child on his back and then plunged to his death from "a considerable height." Some people have attributed the act to Almeron Dickinson, even though he had no son. Others believe it might have been Anthony Wolfe (or Woolf), whose two sons also perished with him in the Alamo.

Regardless of where the story came from, *Shrine of Texas Liberty* is the only film that refers to it at all. In this film, the father is carrying the son on his back when a single bullet brings them down. Come to think of it, virtually every Alamo defender in this low-budget curiosity seems to be brought down by a single bullet, always fired at a distance from a very slow and methodical Mexican soldier.

As times changed, Susannah Dickinson changed, too. She is a fairly conventional suburban-style housewife in both *The Last Command* and

The Alamo (1960)—cooking, cleaning, and taking care of her family. She is a haggard, nearly comatose battle survivor in *Man of Conquest* (1939) and *Gone to Texas* (1986). But she is a full-blown feminist in *The Alamo: 13 Days to Glory* (1987). This feisty Susannah (Kathleen York) makes flags, melts lead for bullets (and even builds a forge to do it with), and mouths off to Santa Anna (Raul Julia). Cocking her head toward the other women survivors, she says, "I ask that you spare their lives. For myself, I would have fought with the men."

Sadly, the various Almeron Dickinsons in the cinema don't change much at all from film to film. John Russell's Dickinson is stoic and determined in *The Last Command*. Bruce Warren's Al is likeable and sincere in *Heroes of the Alamo*. Interestingly, while all the other heroes die rather offhand deaths in this film, only Al gets a certain degree of drama. As the battle nears its end, he goes into the room where Anne and Angelina are hiding. He drinks some water, then embraces his wife for the last time, making her promise to stay where she is. He walks out and is immediately shot. Of course, Anne doesn't stay put, which allows her to cradle Al's head in her arms as he whines out a few last words before dying.

In *The Immortal Alamo,* Almeron Dickinson is both tender and courageous, holding the yarn as his wife knits in one scene, bravely riding for Sam Houston in another, and angrily skewering with his sword the man who has tried to steal his wife in the climactic scene.

In John Wayne's *The Alamo,* Captain Dickinson (Ken Curtis) is more prominent in the Alamo command than any other Dickinson except Bruce Warren in *Heroes of the Alamo*. He serves almost as a second in command to Laurence Harvey's Travis, who—in this film only—is Mrs. Dickinson's cousin. Dickinson is patient with his friend Travis while fully recognizing what a prig he is: "Oh, Will, leave it to you to take it in the worst possible way!" But he is also a decisive military man and a loving, appreciative husband. When Susannah refuses to leave the fort with the other wives, she says, "Don't be angry with me." Dickinson replies, "I'm not angry—I'm proud!" For what it's worth, Ken Curtis is the only singing Dickinson in Alamo movies; he and Joan O'Brien's Susannah croon "Tennessee Babe" to daughter Angelina (Aissa Wayne). And he has the coolest death scene of all Dickinsons: Hit by a bullet, he spins around and falls over a short wooden palisade. His legs catch and

Jules Guerin's romantic view of the Alamo by moonlight appeared in *Ladies' Home Journal*, April 1921. From the collection of Craig R. Covner.

Battle of The Alamo, San Antonio,
Texas, 1836. Painting by F. C. Yohn.

"Since wars begin
in the minds of men,
it is in the minds of men
that the defenses of peace
must be constructed."

—Constitution of *UNESCO*

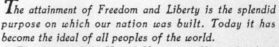

*The attainment of Freedom and Liberty is the splendid
purpose on which our nation was built. Today it has
become the ideal of all peoples of the world.*

*The charter of the United Nations reaffirms this faith
in fundamental human rights, in the dignity and worth
of the individual, in equal opportunity for everyone. Let
us join with other nations in dedicating ourselves—peace-
fully, using only the minds of men—to the high purpose
of a better life for all.*

**America Fore
Loyalty Group**

The Continental Insurance Company • Firemen's Insurance Company of Newark, New Jersey • Fidelity-Phenix Insurance Company
Niagara Fire Insurance Company • The Fidelity and Casualty Company of New York • National-Ben Franklin Insurance Company of Pittsburgh, Pa.
Milwaukee Insurance Company of Milwaukee, Wis. • Commercial Insurance Company of Newark, N. J. • The Yorkshire Insurance Company of New York
Seaboard Fire & Marine Insurance Company • Niagara Insurance Company (Bermuda) Limited • Royal General Insurance Company of Canada

80 MAIDEN LANE, NEW YORK 38, NEW YORK ——— HOME OFFICES ——— 10 PARK PLACE, NEWARK 1, NEW JERSEY

What does the Alamo have to do with life insurance? From the author's collection.

The image of the Alamo has been used not only to promote train travel, but to sell cigars. From the author's collection.

This conceptual painting by Petko Kadiev for the film *Viva Max* shows Alamo Plaza circa 1969. The Alamo no longer looks much like it did during the battle of 1836. From the collection of Craig R. Covner.

Edwin W. Deming's watercolor illustration from *Rise of the Lone Star* (1936). From the author's collection.

A panel from the "Read & Hear Book and Recording" of *Davy Crockett*. This was a comic book that came with a 45-rpm record. From the author's collection.

In this Western comic, the Two-Gun Kid finds that his pal Jim Bowie has died in the Alamo—all because Wolf Fargo and his outlaw gang have cut down the bridge that would have brought reinforcements! Well, it *could* happen. From the author's collection.

A blond Crockett and lots of cavalry soldiers duke it out with Santa Anna's soldiers in these panels from the "Read & Hear Book & Recording" of *Davy Crockett*. From the author's collection.

Caroline Shelton's 1968 watercolor shows an Alamo sitting amid the happy bustle of modern San Antonio. As is so common in Alamo pictures, the dimensions and shapes shown here only barely correspond to those of the real building, yet it is instantly recognizable as the Alamo. From the author's collection.

The 1824 flag always flies over the mythic Alamo, but there is little reason to believe that it flew over the actual one. This battle scene is from the 1961 publication, *Flags of America.* From the collection of Craig R. Covner.

An illustration from *Coronet Magazine*, 1953. From the collection of Paul Andrew Hutton.

A panel from *Davy Crockett* (*Classics Illustrated* no. 129). From the author's collection.

Reynold Brown's poster-art painting for John Wayne's *The Alamo* (1960). Here the Crockett pose is familiar, but Wayne's Davy holds a torch instead of a rifle. Courtesy of Reynold Brown.

In this *True West* cover, Santa Anna takes a far more active role in the attack on the Alamo than he did in real life. Actually, he waited out the battle from his headquarters in San Antonio. From the author's collection.

Mexicans in sombreros attack the Alamo in this vivid battle scene by Howard L. Hastings. This painting served as both cover and frontispiece to the book *Texas: A Romantic Story for Young People*, by J. Walker McSpadden (J. H. Sears & Company, Inc., 1927). From the collection of Craig R. Covner.

A rare poster advertising Frank Hitchcock Murdock's long-running play, *Davy Crockett: or, Be Sure You're Right, Then Go Ahead*, starring Frank Mayo. From the collection of Paul Andrew Hutton.

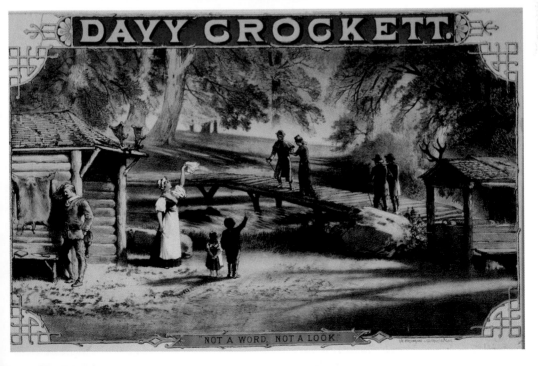

John Wayne tried to film the story of the Alamo for years, even when he was under contract to Republic Pictures. This ad from a trade journal dates from 1948—a full eleven years before Wayne actually produced the film with his own company, Batjac. From the author's collection.

The interior of the Alamo of *Viva Max* (1968), as seen in a conceptual painting by Petko Kadiev. The actual set was built on a soundstage at Cinecitta Studios in Rome. Only the exterior shots of the Alamo were actually filmed in San Antonio. From the collection of Craig R. Covner.

Illustrations to the French edition of *The Alamo,* a novel by Steve Frazee. Though it had nothing to do with the John Wayne film, this book was chosen as the official "novelization." It's a terrific Alamo novel in its own right; if the Wayne *Alamo* had been based on this book, it would undoubtedly have been a much better film. From the collection of Craig R. Covner.

"The Ballad of the Alamo" as recorded by the Sons of Texas. From the author's collection.

The "Build the Alamo" cutout book. From the author's collection.

The colorful header card for a bagged version of the Marx Alamo playset. From the author's collection.

The Waynamo, refurbished for *Alamo ... the Price of Freedom*. Note that the upper windows have been filled in (the outlines are still clearly visible), and that the skyline has been raised slightly. The stone is also substantially darker and dirtier than it appeared in the Wayne film. Photographed by the author.

C. Henry Gordon is a villainous Santa Anna in *Man of Conquest* (1939). Courtesy of Republic Pictures.

J. Carroll Naish is a relatively kind-hearted Santa Anna in *The Last Command* (1955). Courtesy of Republic Pictures.

Julian Rivero as Santa Anna in *Heroes of the Alamo* (1937). From the collection of Paul Andrew Hutton.

Edward James Olmos portrays Santa Anna as angry and vengeful in *Seguin* (1982). From the collection of Paul Andrew Hutton.

his body hangs there, upside down. The stunt was both effective and painful—Curtis pulled a groin muscle while executing it.

Santa Anna

General Antonio Lopez de Santa Anna is also a movie character in constant transition. In *Martyrs of the Alamo* (1915), Walter Long's Santa Anna is cruel and stupid. A title card describes him as an "inveterate drug fiend noted for his shameful orgies." Indeed, as Houston and his vengeful army prepare to attack Santa Anna at San Jacinto, the dictator is kicking back in his tent with several lovely ladies, one of whom is dancing provocatively for him. He is clearly stoned. Because of the negative racial attitudes toward the Mexicans in this film, it may significant that only a few months earlier, Long had played a renegade Black named Gus in Griffith's *Birth of a Nation*. Gus is the evil former slave whose rape attempt drives the pure little Flora (Mae Marsh) to leap off a cliff to her death. Long's Santa Anna is capable of the same kind of outrage, but is too powerful to have to resort to such things.

The Santa Annas of the thirties are more conventional villain types. C. Henry Gordon, in *Man of Conquest* (1939), even has a pencil-thin mustache, all ready for twirling in a sinister manner. While ordering the attack on the Alamo, he says gleefully, "Let's give these Texans something to remember."

In *Heroes of the Alamo* (1937), Julian Rivero's Santa Anna does little but pose, as does Paul Willet's stilted dictator in *Shrine of Texas Liberty* (1938). However, Willet's general is the only cinematic Santa Anna to offer to adopt little Angelina Dickinson, a quaint Alamo legend that seems to be only slightly rooted in fact. (Susannah Dickinson once apparently said that Santa Anna "threatened" to take her and Angelina to Mexico City, which isn't quite the same as adoption.)

By contrast, J. Carrol Naish's Santa Anna in Frank Lloyd's *The Last Command* (1955) is cultured and charming, an honorable leader and businessman protecting his government's interests. He is also a close friend of Jim Bowie's (Sterling Hayden) and is genuinely distressed that the two of them have wound up on opposite sides of the Alamo's walls.

In Jesus Trevino's revisionist production *Seguin* (1982), Edward James Olmos is a snarling, vindictive villain. And in *Alamo ... the Price of Freedom* (1988), Enrique Sandino plays the general as regal, but cal-

Left: Juan Seguin (Joseph Calleia) is depicted in John Wayne's *The Alamo* as the alcalde (mayor) of San Antonio. However, there are a few problems with the Wayne version. First, the real Seguin was only thirty years old at the time of the siege of the Alamo; next, he didn't die in the Alamo (as Calleia's does); and finally, he didn't become alcalde until four years later. Otherwise, perfectly true. Courtesy of Batjac Prod.

Right: Derek Caballero plays Seguin in *Alamo . . . the Price of Freedom* (1988). Courtesy of Rivertheatre Associates.

culating and callous. When one of his officers protests the potential cost in lives should they attack the Alamo, Santa Anna coolly replies, holding up a chicken leg, "The lives of our soldiers are no more important than this chicken."

Only in the television movie *The Alamo: 13 Days to Glory* (1988) has any attempt been made to portray Santa Anna as a brave, complex, ingenious leader as well as a ticking time bomb suffering a personality disorder. Raul Julia (stepping in at the last minute for original casting choice Ricardo Montalban) found both the genius and the madman within Santa Anna; his portrayal conveys something of the character that inspired such fear, awe, and respect in 1836.

The Tejanos

Tejanos have figured much less prominently in Alamo movies. They are generally background figures, if present at all. One fictional Tejano helps carry Ken Tobey's Jim Bowie into his room in the church in *Davy Crockett at the Alamo*. As he is about to leave, the man gestures to an icon in the room and says comfortingly, "Saint Antonio will watch over you." There don't seem to be any Tejano defenders at all in the garrisons of any of the silent-movie Alamos, but there are several prominent ones in what is possibly the most convincing Alamo of all, *Man of Conquest* (1939).

However, both *The Last Command* and Wayne's *The Alamo* seek to make certain that the battle is presented not as an ethnic fight, but as a political one. *The Last Command* includes Juan Seguin (Edward Colmans) among the Alamo garrison, and it invents two other Tejanos: Lorenzo de Quesada (Eduard Franz) and Consuela (Anna Maria Alberghetti). Consuela's romance with Sterling Hayden's Jim Bowie parallels the relationship of Flaca (Linda Cristal) with John Wayne's Davy Crockett. They exist not only to give the films the love interest so necessary for the box office but also to support the view that the fight was not simply Anglo vs. Hispanic. Wayne's film even invents an evil Anglo—Emil Sande (Wesley Lau), who is pro–Santa Anna—as a way to further bring home the point.

Jesus Trevino's *Seguin* told the story entirely from the Tejano point of view; Travis, Bowie, and Crockett barely figure in the film. Trevino's aim was not only to give the Hispanic defenders of the Alamo their due, but to recast the story of the Texas Revolution in a new light. He said, "I was interested in telling the Chicano side of American history which both John Wayne and American textbooks have ignored." Trevino considered his filming location to be an ironic statement in itself: he shot *Seguin* on the John Wayne set in Brackettville, Texas. To some, Trevino's decision to film the story of Juan Seguin was a controversial one. A member of his panel of advisors, Rudy Acuna (a Chicano historian at California State University, Northridge), resigned. Acuna protested that Trevino was attempting to "make heroes of the Mexican people defending the Alamo," which was, he said, "like making heroes of the Vichy government."[1]

The debut of the IMAX film, *Alamo . . . the Price of Freedom* (1988),

The racial tensions that continue to surround the Alamo were given a comic twist in the 1968 film *Viva Max,* based on the book by James Lehrer. In it, an inept Mexican general (Peter Ustinov) and his ragtag army occupy the Alamo, claiming it Mexican property. The film spoofs many of the Alamo legends, but as General Max finds meaning in his gesture—and his men unite to stand with him—it ultimately becomes a true Alamo movie. Courtesy of Republic Pictures.

was met by passionate and vocal protests from Hispanic groups, who complained that once again in the Alamo story, the Tejanos were being ignored and the Mexican army demonized. San Antonio city council member Walter Martinez read an early draft of the script and was outraged, claiming that the Tejanos were depicted as "subservient" and "less heroic than their non-Hispanic counterparts." He told a *Los*

Angeles Times reporter, "If we are unhappy with the film in any way, we will ask the producers to remove objectionable scenes. The bottom line is, if we cannot come to an agreement on objectionable scenes, we plan to boycott the film."[2] George McAlister, the film's producer and screenwriter, was quoted in the same article: "The film, a docudrama, is not degrading to Hispanics or anyone. We treat Santa Anna's soldiers and the Tejanos with great sensitivity."[3]

Local Hispanic leaders were shown a seventy-eight-minute-long rough cut (the final film was about forty-eight minutes long). They saw a poor-quality videocassette, but it wasn't just the image they disliked. They complained that the film was "amateurish," "boring," and "slow."

Which, of course, it was. But it's difficult to look at the film and see any kind of racial bias at work. The Tejano defenders of the Alamo are prominent in the film. And the soldiers and officers of Santa Anna are portrayed only in the most positive light of courage and integrity. As in all Alamo movies, Santa Anna is the one true bad guy; but even here, he is not pure evil. He is simply an arrogant leader who cares little for the lives of his men, whom he considers little more than cannon fodder.

Even so, *Price of Freedom*'s protestors had a point. When Davy Crockett strides on-screen, he doesn't have to say anything or do anything; everyone in the audience knows exactly who he is. But when Toribio Losoyo and Gregorio Esparza amble onto center screen without introduction, the effect isn't enlightening at all. Who are they? Why are they here? When Losoyo says in *Price of Freedom*, "I was born in the Alamo and I'll die in the Alamo," what does he mean? Unfortunately, the answers are not in the film; they must be learned elsewhere. Certainly this is a failure of length rather than intention, but the protestors' ultimate point is still not addressed. When will the Tejano members of the Alamo garrison stand beside their Anglo brothers in myth, as well as in history?

James Bowie

Among the most problematic of the major players in the Alamo myth is James Bowie. He was a legendary fighting man. He didn't invent the Bowie knife, but he certainly made it famous. His incredibly adventurous life encompassed notorious knife fights and Indian battles. He smuggled contraband and traded slaves with Jean Laffite and searched

Above: Bowie (Roger Williams) struggles out of his cot to make his last stand in *Heroes of the Alamo*. From the author's collection.

Right: Bowie (Robert Armstrong) takes a Mexican soldier with him in *Man of Conquest* (1939). Courtesy of Republic Pictures.

Is that a Bowie knife, or are you just happy to see me? Alan Ladd as Jim Bowie in *The Iron Mistress* (1953). With him are Virginia Mayo (left) and Phyllis Kirk. Courtesy of Warner Bros.

Left: Ken Tobey's Bowie doesn't cower like this in "Davy Crockett at the Alamo" (1955). He dies fighting on his cot, as legend demands. Courtesy of Walt Disney Prod.

Below: Jim Bowie (Richard Widmark) is about to die with a loud squawk in John Wayne's *The Alamo* (1960). His former slave, Jethro (Jester Hairston), a fictional character, sticks with him to the bitter end. Courtesy of Batjac Prod.

This grisly scene was cut from *Alamo . . . the Price of Freedom*. Bowie's death is shown only in silhouette. Courtesy of Rivertheatre Associates.

for the elusive silver mines of San Saba. He married Ursula de Veramendi, an aristocratic member of one of San Antonio's first families, and he became a powerful landowner. And after all this, he wound up involved in one of the most famous last stands in history.

The trouble is, from a dramatic point of view, Bowie didn't do much in the Alamo except cough. Stricken early in the siege with a disease "of a peculiar nature" (possibly pneumonia or tuberculosis), Bowie was weak and bedridden for most of those thirteen days of glory.

Because of this, Bowie is a relatively minor figure in most of the early Alamo films. He is a dandy in *Martyrs of the Alamo* (1915), dusting off a chair with his handkerchief before sitting down. But later, he is racked with coughs, and awaits his end in bed. In *Davy Crockett at the Fall of the Alamo* (1926), Bowie barely registers as a character, coolly brandishing a rather tiny version of his famous knife early on, and then taking to bed where he remains, except when Travis and Crockett help him stagger across Travis's famous line in the sand. Bowie is a drunken lout in *Alamo . . . the Price of Freedom* (1988) and *James A. Michener's "Texas"* (1994), and a relatively bad-tempered thug in nearly everything else.

In fact, the only Alamo movies that have been able to make anything out of Bowie at all are those that simply ignore his illness. Both *The Last Command* (1955) and *The Alamo: 13 Days to Glory* (1987) attribute his illness to an accident. And the snarling Bowie in John Wayne's *The*

Alamo ("My God, Bowie, you're bad tempered!") just won't get into his cot, although he's repeatedly hurt in a horse fall, by a cannon blast . . . As the final battle is nearing its end, they *finally* move him into the chapel so that he can die (with a loud squawk) on his cot, as his iconography demands.

The rivalry between Bowie and Travis has been emphasized in several of the films. They are at each other's throats in *Martyrs of the Alamo*—in fact, their men hate each other, too, just because they're part of opposing factions. And in both *The Alamo* (1960) and *The Alamo: 13 Days to Glory,* they hate each other so much that they plan to fight a duel to the death. That is, if they survive the battle. There is little historical basis for this enmity. When Bowie and his men had a liquor-soaked party in February 1836, Travis wrote primly that he wouldn't be "responsible for the drunken irregularities of any man." But once they began co-commanding the Alamo—Bowie over the volunteers, Travis over the regulars—they seem to have gotten along just fine. And so they do in most of the films. Travis (Don Megowan) treats Bowie (Kenneth Tobey) with a kind of hushed awe in *Davy Crockett, King of the Wild Frontier* (1955). And they have an easy, laconic camaraderie in *The Man from the Alamo* (1953). Bowie (Stuart Randall) says, "No need to fret, Bill. You can always run if things get too tough." Travis (Arthur Space) replies, "Now, you weren't planning on leaving, were you?" The bedridden Bowie says, "No, I guess not. I don't figure I can run too good." Travis smiles and says, "I don't run good either, Jim."

Though Bowie and Crockett are the most famous names in the Alamo siege, Travis is nearly always the central character of the Alamo films. Travis usually initiates the trouble, commands the fort, and makes the decisions about how to proceed. And it is he who articulates to the men the very meaning of their sacrifice.

William B. Travis

William Barret Travis was twenty-seven years old when he fought and died at the Alamo. Travis was born in South Carolina and had lived for a while in Alabama. In the films, he is nearly always played by an older man, and is only rarely depicted as a Southerner. Most films portray him as not only the best-educated man in the fort but also the most arrogant. In *The Alamo,* Laurence Harvey's Travis refers to his men as "rabble"

Travis (Richard Carlson) dies with a single bullet to the forehead in *The Last Command* (1955). Except that he dies on the south wall instead of the north wall, the depiction is relatively accurate. Courtesy of Republic Pictures.

Laurence Harvey's Travis in *The Alamo* is an arrogant prig—at one point Bowie (Richard Widmark) calls him "a prissy jackass"—who looks down on his men, both literally and figuratively. Courtesy of Batjac Prod.

Alec Baldwin as a hotheaded young Travis in *The Alamo: 13 Days to Glory* (1987). Photograph by Tony Pasqua.

Casey Biggs's Travis in *Alamo . . . the Price of Freedom* (1988) is serious and resolute. Courtesy of Rivertheatre Associates.

and frankly states that he is better than they are. He always looks down on them, literally as well as figuratively. Only at the end, when he offers his men the chance to stay or go, does he stand on the ground and look them square in the face for the first time.[4]

Travis is also something of a pill in *The Last Command* and in *The Alamo: 13 Days to Glory*. In both cases, he gets his priorities straight and is complimented by Bowie on how much he has grown. But the Alamo commander isn't always depicted in this way. Travis is easy-tempered and unsure of himself in *Davy Crockett, King of the Wild Frontier*, decent but troubled in *Alamo . . . the Price of Freedom*, and reluctant to go to war in *Heroes of the Alamo*.

No matter how Travis is depicted, he nearly always has two moments to shine in the Alamo legend—though not always in the Alamo films. First is his famous letter of February 24, 1836 "To the people of Texas and all Americans in the world . . . " This powerful and moving appeal is, astonishingly, almost never used in Alamo movies. When it is, as in *The Alamo: 13 Days to Glory*, it's usually moved to a more dramatic moment in the siege, toward the end. Only *Alamo . . . the Price of Freedom* puts the letter in its proper historical context and gives it the emotional power it deserves. As Travis (Casey Biggs) writes, we see a montage of scenes depicting the mounting siege. We hear the letter in voice-over, accompanied by some of the most powerful passages in Merrill Jenson's musical score.

The second big moment for Travis is his drawing of the famous line in the sand. The line is the most cherished of Alamo legends, even if it is drawn on very shaky historical ground. But whether it really happened, the line is the central moment in the Alamo myth and in all Alamo films—even the comic *Viva Max*. As different as the approach of each Alamo film may be, they all have in common a theme of democratic bonding. The decision of the men to stay in the Alamo is never depicted as mass suicide, although some revisionist historians have chosen to see it in that light. Instead it is shown as a moment when all the men, no matter their background or personalities or political beliefs, choose to join together and act as one.

For such a crucial scene, it's surprising how many Alamo films have nearly thrown the moment away, and how many oddball variations there are. Travis draws the line with the butt of his rifle in *Heroes of the Alamo* and with the heel of his boot in *Davy Crockett at the Fall of the*

The Alamo's holy trinity, Travis (Grant Show), Crockett (John Schneider), and Bowie (David Keith) in *James A. Michener's "Texas"* (1994). Courtesy of Republic Pictures.

Alamo (General Max does it the same way in *Viva Max*). Otherwise, Travis always uses his trusty sabre.

The drawing of the line is always a good time for movie Travises to sum up the theme of their particular movie. "This is not about land or money," says Alec Baldwin's Travis in *The Alamo: 13 Days to Glory,* with an eye toward the yuppies in his eighties audience who believed that everything was. "If I am destined to die," says Casey Biggs's militaristic, Reagan-era Travis in *Alamo . . . the Price of Freedom,* "let my scabbard be empty and my sword red with the blood of men who would deny my freedom."

Moses Rose

In each case, the men of the Alamo cross the line without hesitation—even Jim Bowie, who has to be carried across on his cot. The men of Alamo movies always choose death—all except Moses Rose, the man who leaves, the one Alamo defender who confirms the true democratic nature of the line by voting no. Of course, Rose is far too explosive and controversial a figure to show up in most Alamo films at all. A man is seen to hang back while the others cross the line in *Martyrs of the Alamo,* but he is never specifically identified, nor is his gesture singled out or explained. In *Alamo . . . the Price of Freedom,* Rose says that he's not prepared to die "and will not do so if I can help it," and he exits, screen left, with a flourish.

The character of Rose has been given depth only on television. In *Alamo: 13 Days to Glory,* he is depicted as principled and brave—he just doesn't see this cause as one worth dying for. In the "Siege of the Alamo" episode of the TV series *You Are There* (1971), Rose is shown to be a veteran soldier who has escaped death too many times to willingly acquiesce to it here. And in "The Jose Morales Story," an evocative episode of *Wagon Train* in 1960, Rose is fictionalized as a man who deserted the Alamo years earlier and has been eaten up with shame ever since. When faced with the opportunity to give his life for others, he gladly seizes the chance to find the martyr's grave he missed so long ago.

Davy Crockett

But to the public at large, one Alamo hero has always towered above all the rest: Davy, Davy Crockett, King of the Wild Frontier.

Physically, the old "half-horse, half-alligator" changes very little from film to film. The popular (and crude) Crockett Almanacs had already given the public the essentials of Davy's dress—buckskin clothes and a fur hat made out of some wild animal or other. The stage popularity of Nimrod Wildfire and Frank Mayo's Davy Crockett further cemented the image into the nation's consciousness. It has even been suggested that Crockett himself began to assume some of the characteristics of the already-legendary Davy just because he realized that his public expected it.

By the time the movies discovered Davy Crockett in 1909 (*Davy Crockett—in Hearts United* seems to be the first Crockett film), his image was set and would never change to any degree. Crockett is a solemn ex-congressman in *Davy Crockett at the Fall of the Alamo* (1926), a grizzled, good-natured yarn spinner in *The Last Command* (1955), and a raucous thug, itching for a fight—any fight—in *Heroes of the Alamo* (1937). John Wayne's Crockett in *The Alamo* (1960) is a self-invention, an educated and articulate man who has the politician's ability to adapt his manner to any occasion. And Fess Parker's Davy—the

Left: Fess Parker, the once and future Davy. Courtesy of Walt Disney Prod.

Below: On the set of *The Alamo* (l. to r.) Richard Widmark (Jim Bowie), producer-director John Wayne (Davy Crockett), and director John Ford, Wayne's mentor. From the collection of Joseph Musso.

John Wayne entertains members of the DRT on the set of *The Alamo*. The organization wholeheartedly supported Wayne's mythic version of the events. Eight years later, while the irreverent Alamo comedy *Viva Max* was being filmed, one of the Daughters plaintively asked, "Why can't they make a nice movie, like John Wayne?" From the author's collection.

once and future Davy—in *Davy Crockett, King of the Wild Frontier* (1955) is a noble and moral icon who must do what he thinks is right, no matter the cost.

Besides John Wayne, the only actor who really touched on Crockett's conscious transformation from the congressman to the frontiersman is Cullen Landis, in *Davy Crockett at the Fall of the Alamo*. Early in the film, Crockett arrives at his Tennessee home, resplendent in tailed coat, top hat, and flowered cravat. He learns that he has lost his seat in Congress. He is stung by the news, but tells his friends, "I'm through with politics and Texas needs me." He goes inside and breaks out the buckskins; he has decided to stop being David and get back to being Davy.

Laurence Harvey's Travis in *The Alamo* recognizes the same duality in John Wayne's Crockett: "The bad grammar is a pose," he says. "You speak an excellent and concise English when you wish." Fess Parker's Crockett also served in Congress, but the point of that film was that he

The heroes of the Alamo are treated like icons—literally—in this page from the original pressbook to *Davy Crockett at the Fall of the Alamo* (1926). From the author's collection.

didn't change his essential Davy-ness for Congress. When he goes in to blast them about thwarting his beloved Indian bill, he wears buckskins and speaks without pretension.

Arthur Hunnicutt in *The Last Command* is one of the movies' liveliest Crocketts. While most movies, for some reason, tend to portray Crockett as rather dour, Hunnicutt is a "speechifier" and a humorist. When he first arrives in San Antonio the men ask him to give a speech, and Crockett immediately launches into one: "I been persuaded." Best of all, he isn't overly heroic: "That Santa Anna 'bout scares me to death." When Bowie (Sterling Hayden) is hurt in a fall and incapacitated, Crockett worries less about Bowie's health than about the effect it will have on the men. "We need him," Davy says. "We need the idea of him." Spoken like a man who understands that the men of the Alamo need the *idea* of Crockett more than they need Crockett himself.

In *Heroes of the Alamo,* Lane Chandler's Davy is younger than he

Left: Some of the posters for *Davy Crockett at the Fall of the Alamo* (1926). *Right:* Poster for *Man of Conquest (1939).* From the author's collection.

ought to be, but otherwise an interesting mixture of fact and fancy. When he arrives at the fort, he isn't even quite sure why he's there. "Well, this is the nearest fight I could find. You see, Travis, it's a long story, but the meat of it's this: the numbskull voters in Tennessee wouldn't send me back to Congress for another term. And I figured your little war here was the next best thing to Congress."

Travis (Rex Lease) replies, "Well, if it's fightin' you're lookin' for you may get an overdose with us."

Crockett is puzzled by this. "Overdose? Let's see, it's Mexicans you're fightin', ain't it? Oh well, doesn't matter. One fight's just like another to me and old Betsy here. I reckon I'll stay and help."

No Crockett of the movies surrenders and is executed, as some historians now believe the real Crockett did. They all go down most hero-

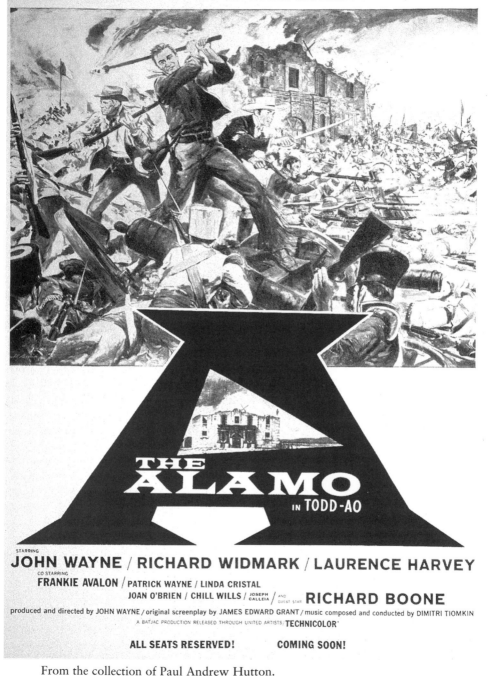

From the collection of Paul Andrew Hutton.

Although Crockett is prominently featured in this ad for the science fiction TV series "The Time Tunnel" (1966), he doesn't appear in the show itself. When the hapless time travelers arrive at the Alamo on March 6, they are offhandedly informed that "Crockett was killed yesterday." Forget de la Pena—now *this* is revisionism! From the collection of Paul Andrew Hutton.

ically, swingin' Ol' Betsy like Fess Parker, or blowing themselves to kingdom come like John Wayne and Arthur Hunnicutt, or duking it out mano a mano with the Mexicans like Cullen Landis. Only Lane Chandler's Davy dies in a relatively non-heroic way. At the end of the battle, Santa Anna (Julian Rivero) enters the fort for a look-see. Something catches his eye. It's Crockett, painfully crawling on the ground. Santa Anna points and growls, "Kill that!" A Mexican soldier strolls over and clubs Davy in the head with the butt of his rifle. Then, thanks to the miracle of bad writing and worse direction, Crockett clutches his *chest,* defiantly says something like, "I'll be dang to ya!" and dies. Did I say non-heroic? Maybe non-*sense* is the better word.

Too Bad They're Not Better

The Alamo movies share one unfortunate trait. None of them is much good. There doesn't seem to be a good reason for this, but here's a possibility: The Alamo has not yet been approached by a screenwriter or director who chose to treat it as anything but a foregone conclusion. From the moment any Alamo film opens, these are dead men; we're just waiting around to see how they die. A truly great Alamo film will never be made without characters who believe they are headed for something *beyond* the Alamo. Their deaths should be an interruption, a tragedy. The audience should be gripped with dread as the end approaches because they know—as the characters should not—how badly it will all end.

The other major problem with the Alamo, of course, is that the siege is basically about waiting. The Texans and Mexicans don't really fight each other until the very end; they don't even parley with each other very much. As long as Alamo movies stick to the holy trinity of Crockett, Travis, and Bowie, they're going to be stuck behind walls, not doing much until the big blowout at the end. John Wayne tried to give his film some action. But his men could come and go from the Alamo so easily— stealing cattle, blowing up a big cannon—that their decision to stay and die in the fort is completely nonsensical. Bowie (Richard Widmark) constantly urges Crockett and Travis to join with him in a guerilla action— "Cut, slash, and run!"—and, in the context of the film, he's absolutely right. When they hit the enemy by surprise, they always win. When they elect to stand with Travis and die in the Alamo, it doesn't seem like a transcendent moment of bravery; it seems like they're giving up, with no compelling reason. Wayne tried to have his cake and eat it by having the men of the Alamo under siege, but still able to waltz in and out of the Alamo whenever they like—and that's only one reason his film fails so miserably at depicting the reality of the Alamo.

Other, probably most, Alamo films have failed as miserably. Looked at in the cold light of day, they mostly seem inadequate as drama and virtually empty of history.

But taken together, in almost every Alamo film we can find moving, sometimes beautiful moments. None entirely works on its own, but in the aggregate, they make one big, powerful (albeit flawed) Alamo movie: A movie that is entertaining, sometimes inspiring, and illuminated—occasionally—by bright flashes of truth.

Two Lost Alamo Films—and an Alamo Mystery

The first film about the battle of the Alamo came about as an indirect result of the price of leather in Europe.

Georges Melies was one of the founding fathers of the cinema. An innovator and stylist almost without peer, Melies helped to create a grammar of film. A magician, he saw the cinema as the perfect extension of fantastic stagecraft. The whimsical and wildly imaginative films made by Melies in France between 1896 and 1913 have not lost their power to enchant and entertain a century after they were first made. His company, Star Films, carried one of the first trademarks in movie history.

Georges's brothers, Gaston and Henri, managed the London branch of the Melies shoe factory. In 1893, they entered into a deal with the French war ministry, which transformed the business into a joint-stock company, of which Gaston was the manager. The deal, which called for Gaston to supply boots to the military, was to have lasted for six years. But the price of leather increased

Gaston Melies, head of the Star Film Company. Here, he's in costume for his role as a padre in *The Immortal Alamo*. From the author's collection.

suddenly in January 1895, and Gaston was forced to shut down the factory. In August, the war ministry cancelled the contract. Gaston was ruined.

Because of his business experience, Gaston soon found another managerial job: taking care of Georges's motion picture compa-

Hot Wells Hotel in San Antonio, Texas. This photograph was taken in about 1910—just when the Star Film Company arrived there. From the author's collection.

ny. It may have been slightly galling for Gaston to find himself employed by his little brother, but under his guidance, the Star Film Company flourished.

Several years later, when Georges's copyright problems in the United States became overwhelming, he asked Gaston to go to New York to set things right. Gaston was happy to do so, for at least two reasons: The new post would put some distance between the brothers, granting Gaston far more autonomy than he enjoyed in France; and Gaston was still grieving from the death of his wife Augustine (in July 1901). New York offered him a much-needed fresh start.

But once in New York, Gaston decided to begin making films himself. The fantastic films that Georges made were meticulously crafted, a process that was time-consuming and expensive. Gaston decided to make films with commerce in mind, not art. He began with newsreels and other actualities, but eventually began filming simple dramas and comedies.

In those days, films were normally made outdoors and lit only by sunlight. In the winter, the New York and New Jersey companies looked for warmer, sunnier places to film. Some went south to Florida, others west to Oregon and California. Gaston Melies chose San Antonio, Texas. In January 1910, the Star Film Company set up shop at a leased

The Dickinsons are the main characters of this one-reel film. They were played by Edith Storey and William Carroll. From the author's collection.

The defenders and their families enter the Alamo. From the author's collection.

Dickinson is sent to Sam Houston for help. From the author's collection.

farmhouse just across the river from Hot Wells Hotel, a famous sulphur springs resort. There, over the next year, Star Films produced some seventy comedies, dramas, and Westerns.

A motion picture about the Alamo was one of the first projects discussed upon the Star Film Company's arrival in San Antonio. However, it was actually one of the last filmed, due partly to the relative complexity of the plot and the ambitious nature of the film. By Star Film standards, a movie that utilized nearly one hundred extras qualified as an epic. *The Immortal Alamo* was without exception the biggest, most expensive, most important film the company produced in Texas, or anywhere else.

The Immortal Alamo was written and conceived by Wilbert Melville, described in *The Film Index* as "a well known theatrical writer. He is familiar with Texas topography, having been in that section in advance of theatrical attractions; and so his dramas and comedies have been written with an eye to utilizing the best that Texas could afford."[5] Melville had the task of boiling down into a single reel of film the thirteen-day siege of the Alamo, the vengeful battle of San Jacinto, *and* a romantic subplot.

In *The Immortal Alamo*, the story centers on Susannah (called "Lucy" here) and Almeron Dickinson, who with their daughter Angelina formed one of the families in the Alamo during the siege. In the movie, a villainous Mexican named Navarre lusts after Lucy. When the Mexican army arrives in San Antonio and the Texans take refuge inside the Alamo, Col. Travis sends Lt. Dickinson to Sam Houston for aid. Once Dickinson is out of the way, Navarre makes his move on Lucy, who angrily rebuffs him. Travis orders Navarre out of the Alamo.

In spite, Navarre goes to Santa Anna and tells him how few defenders are inside and how desperate is their situation. As a reward, he asks to have his pick of the surviving females. After the massacre, Navarre chooses Lucy

The attack begins. From the author's collection.

for his bride. Just as he is about to force her to marry him, Houston, Dickinson, and the Texans arrive—like the cavalry, at the last moment—defeating the Mexican army in no time. Dickinson kills Navarre, and Santa Anna surrenders.

As with the Alamo films that followed it (and equally falsely), the producers of *The Immortal Alamo* made extravagant claims about the level of research that went into bringing the epic to the screen. The film, one article claimed, would be

> taken at the actual spot where [the battle] took place. All the data relating to this siege has been obtained from direct descendants of the illustrious warriors who sacrificed their lives in fighting for their country during this siege. These native Texans, who are thoroughly imbued with the intense patriotism with which their forefathers were inspired, have entered into this remarkable work of the Melies company and are extending every help and giving their most eager interest and assistance in reconstructing this great historical event. Everywhere the company has been supplied with information and

documents which will make this series of historical events unique in the annals of moving picture photography. The company has covered the ground most thoroughly to the Mexican border, and has lived over again the experiences of those who fought for the freedom of the Lone Star state.[6]

The "actual spot" of which the writer speaks probably referred to San Antonio in general, not the Alamo in particular. But it is possible that at least part of *The Immortal Alamo* was actually filmed at the shrine. Although acknowledging that the Alamo of 1911 did not resemble the Alamo of 1836, Gaston petitioned the mayor of San Antonio for permission to film *The Immortal Alamo* on the grounds of the shrine. The Daughters of the Republic of Texas, caretakers of the Alamo since 1906, controlled the interior of the church and refused to allow the filmmakers inside. But the city owned the public square; and the mayor, possibly recognizing an unprecedented opportunity to bring the attention of audiences all over the world to San Antonio, finally granted permission. Because *The*

The interior of the Alamo. Lucy Dickinson (Edith Storey) tries to comfort a dejected Travis (William Clifford). From the author's collection.

Santa Anna's army was portrayed by cadets from the Peacock Military Academy in San Antonio. From the author's collection.

After the battle, the evil Navarre (Francis Ford) claims Lucy for his own. From the author's collection.

Immortal Alamo no longer exists, it is difficult to determine exactly what was filmed at the Alamo itself. Surviving photographs show a detailed painted backdrop of the Alamo, making it easy to infer that the actual building was never used.

But one trade publication report proves that inference wrong—and, incidentally, gives us at least an approximate date of the film's production:

> In the face of bad weather, the streets of San Antonio around the Alamo being crowded for the Cattlemen's Convention, the mobilization of the troops in San Antonio, and other causes, it was difficult to take pictures of the celebrated building and keep the crowds back for the grouping of the characters. But it was finally done to the satisfaction of the director, Mr. Gaston Melies, who was actively in charge of the work.[7]

The Cattlemen's Convention was held in San Antonio the week of March 19–24, 1911, and attracted so many thousands of delegates that nearly every business and place of amusement in the city was swelled with their ranks. All that marred the festivities were constant showers, which drenched the city all week long. Because of these clues, we know—within a week—when *The Immortal Alamo* was filmed. Its release date of May 25 confirms this; in those days it usually took about two months for a film to reach the screen.

But exactly what was this "grouping of the characters" that Gaston was trying to capture on film? We may never know for sure. However, since the painted backdrop was used for the film's action sequences, perhaps it refers to a modern-day coda to the story in front of the real Alamo.

Gaston approached the famous Peacock Military Academy for the loan of about one hundred cadets. This was probably because their parade uniforms—shakos, long-tailed blue coats, and white pants—were close enough to the Mexican uniforms of 1836 to get by. By and large the cadets were kept in the background, so that their youth was not too apparent on-screen.

It isn't known where the interior scenes were filmed, but it is logical to assume that they were set up in the ruins of one of the missions. These settings mix theatrical backdrops with real stone

Just as Navarre is about to force Lucy into a sham marriage, Houston's vengeful army arrives. Dickinson kills Navarre. From the author's collection.

walls and rubble. Since these "interiors" would have to have been filmed outside, the inside of the Alamo could well have been an open section of Mission San Jose, perhaps its roofless chapel.

Because of the size of the production, nearly every member of the company was called into service to play at least one role in *The Immortal Alamo*; some actors might have played multiple parts. William Clifford played Travis, Edith Storey and William Carroll played Lucy and Lt. Dickinson, and Francis Ford, the elder brother of famed director John Ford, played the villain, Navarre.

There were also some performers on view who weren't professional actors. The padre who conducts the forced marriage between Navarre and Lucy was played by none other than Gaston Melies himself. As one reporter wrote:

It developed during the posing of the picture that every available actor, cowboy and ranch hand, together with a hundred students of the Peacock Military College, were in the uniforms of the opposing forces, and a priest was necessary. The sun was getting low, the director [William Haddock] knew that he must make haste to finish this picture or call the entire staff on the following day. In this emergency Mr. Melies was coaxed to play the padre. Always with a keen eye for the makeup that would photograph well, he constructed the one used in the film. And his admiring company, which had never seen him save as persona propria, prevailed upon him to pose for . . . photographs.[8]

That the filmmakers played fast and loose with history proved to be too much for *New York Dramatic Mirror* reader Paul H. McGregor of Temple,

Santa Anna surrenders to Sam Houston. From the author's collection.

Texas. "They butchered history," he wrote, "to give it a cheap appearance. Lieutenant Dickinson was not at the battle of San Jacinto, but perished in the Alamo. Would not this true history have made a stronger play than to butcher sacred history in order to have the hero stab the villain and catch the heroine in his arms? Mockery!"[9]

The critics didn't agree with Mr. McGregor, feeling that history and fiction had been expertly and imperceptibly merged:

The historical societies of Texas contributed their share to make the picture correct in every detail and this really should prove to

be one of the sensations of the present year. The romance has been blended so closely with the story of the siege and fall of the Alamo that its benefit as a historical subject has been enhanced by the attractiveness with which the story is presented.[10]

★ ★ ★

Today, *The Immortal Alamo* is lost. The only visual evidence that survives is a handful of photographs. But at least five images that have always been accepted as representing scenes from *The Immortal Alamo* are actually from *another* lost Alamo movie.

The first time I ever heard of

The Immortal Alamo was when I read about it in Don Graham's excellent book, *Cowboys and Cadillacs: How Hollywood Looks at Texas* (Texas Monthly Press, 1983). On page 10 of that book, Graham offers up a full-page portrait of an actor in coonskin cap and buckskins, holding a flintlock rifle. The caption reads in part, "The actor is Francis Ford."

About three years later, *Texas Monthly* magazine's November 1986 issue featured a cover story by Paul Andrew Hutton, titled "Davy Crockett, Still King of the Wild Frontier." On page 125, a "Coonskin Hall of Fame" celebrates several great movie Crocketts, including Francis Ford. The same still photo is printed there as in Graham's book. On page 128 is a battle scene, purported to be from *The Immortal Alamo*. It shows "Francis Ford" as Davy, lying dead on the floor while a woman tries to fight off a Mexican soldier who is about to do in a bedridden Jim Bowie. In a corner, a woman cowers with a baby— obviously a Susannah Dickinson character.

In 1987, I spent several weeks in San Antonio researching the book that would eventually be published in 1991 as *Alamo Movies*. The first thing I asked for at the DRT Library on the Alamo grounds was to see whatever stills they might have from *The Immortal Alamo*. Their file contained four stills: the two I had already seen, a shot of Crockett fighting off Mexicans (with a sword!), and a shot of several too-modern cowboys firing rifles into the smoke.

Happily, I rounded up several more photographs from the film in the next couple of years, so by the time my book was published, I could feature a whopping thirteen images from *The Immortal Alamo*. I had, in the meantime, seen the same DRT stills in other articles, always identified as being from *The Immortal Alamo*.

But from the beginning, something troubled me about some of the shots. During the production phase of *Alamo Movies*, I remember sitting and staring at the stills, comparing a photograph of Francis Ford from the period with the picture of Crockett. They looked completely different, but everything in print, everything anyone had ever written on the subject, confirmed that it was Ford. The thought that everyone might be wrong just couldn't quite penetrate my thick skull.

That is, until right after the book was published. One day, I

Who is this Crockett? A production still for, perhaps, *The Siege and Fall of the Alamo* (1913). From the author's collection.

just glanced at one of the stills that was indisputably from the film and recognized Francis Ford standing in the background. He wasn't Crockett—he was the villain Navarre! So I spent hours going through all the photographs of Star Film Ranch actors trying to match up somebody, anybody, with the Crockett portrait. I was unsuccessful.

Then in 1998, Martha Utterback from the DRT Library sent me three photographs of the real Alamo. A wooden palisade had been built on the southwest corner, and the photographs seemed to indicate that a film was being made. I was ecstatic. I thought I was looking at production stills of the very first Alamo movie.

But I wasn't.

In one of the stills, the Alamo long barracks could be seen. There was no second floor. Knowing that the remaining fragments of the second story had been knocked down in 1913 (see Chapter Four), I realized that the film in progress was not *The Immortal Alamo*. In fact, the palisade in those stills matches perfectly with the one our mystery Crockett is posed in front of. So not only is this Crockett not Francis Ford, he's not even from *The Immortal Alamo*—which means that the other three related stills from the DRT files aren't from *The Immortal Alamo,* either.

So, what are the stills from? It's difficult to be absolutely certain, with no other corresponding evidence, but they seem to be from *The Siege and Fall of the Alamo,* a film that we know to have been made on location in San Antonio in 1914. *The Siege and Fall of the Alamo* opened at San Antonio's Royal Theater on June 1, 1914. The next day, an ad that appeared in the *San Antonio Light* revealed that the film had

Original stock certificate for the "Siege and Fall of the Alamo Motion Picture Company." From the author's collection.

From the author's collection.

been produced locally, had cost $35,000, and was five reels long—making it the first feature-length film about the Alamo. A synopsis survives (barely) in the Library of Congress, but it tells us little about what the film might have been like. And there is no indication there or elsewhere as to who made the film or who was in it. So the mystery Crockett is still a mystery. That's doubly sad, since it might actually have been good. The *San Antonio Light* called it "a splendid piece of photography, clear in every

The Alamo in 1914, with a palisade attached for *The Siege and Fall of the Alamo*. This may be the only film about the 1836 battle in which the Alamo played itself. Courtesy of DRT Library, the Alamo.

detail, and the acting is perfect. The play seems to please the patrons and is pronounced by historians as a great production."[11] That's more than can be said for just about any other Alamo film.

So, we now have fewer images from the lost *The Immortal Alamo* than we thought we did. But, on the bright side, we now have *four* stills, and at least three production shots, of another lost Alamo movie. Now, if only an actual print of either of these films would show up . . .

Crockett kills many Mexicans—with a sabre, not Ol' Betsy. From the author's collection.

The Mexican soldiers return the favor. And while they're at it, they kill Bowie, too. Always identified as scenes from *The Immortal Alamo* (1911), these are probably from *The Siege and Fall of the Alamo* (1913). From the author's collection.

Fun and Games: Alamo Toys, Songs, and Souvenirs

March 6, 1836 is the most important date related to the historical Alamo, but perhaps the day with the most significance for Alamo pop-culture enthusiasts is December 15, 1954. It was on this evening that "Davy Crockett, Indian Fighter" first aired on Walt Disney's new *Disneyland* television series. "Davy Crockett, Indian Fighter" was the first of a three-part series on the frontier figure: "Davy Crockett Goes to Congress" aired on January 26, 1955, and "Davy Crockett at the Alamo" followed on February 24, 1955.

Intended only as low-budget episodic TV filler, the three "Crockett" episodes fueled a national craze that would sweep the nation with a furor that wouldn't be matched until the Beatles' arrival a decade later. Disney's Crockett craze delivered the Alamo from the dusty pages of history and turned it into an icon of pop culture. Its young star, Fess Parker, had appeared in only a couple of films, but his genial portrayal of the legendary "half-horse, half-alligator" transformed him into a major star. To kids everywhere, Parker *was*—as the theme song claimed—Davy Crockett, King of the Wild Frontier.

In 1954, only a few films and television shows were accompanied by merchandising campaigns of the kind we are so accustomed to today. The overwhelming response to the Crockett series caught the Disney organization off-guard—but only momentarily. Within weeks, the market was flooded with Crockett tie-ins of incredible number and variety, more than any single kid could ever hope to own. Walt Disney Productions authorized hundreds of "Official Davy Crockett" items:

marionettes, bedsheets, table lamps, tricycles, lunch boxes, costumes, knives, guns, pajamas, dinnerware—almost everything imaginable. Of course, one of the most popular items was the coonskin cap. The caps came in brown for boys and white "Polly Crockett" coonskins for girls, and they nearly did to America's raccoon population what Santa Anna did to the men at the Alamo.

The ubiquitous theme song, "The Ballad of Davy Crockett"—tossed off in about twenty minutes by composer George Bruns and screenwriter and novelist Tom Blackburn—became an enormous hit by any standards. Some sixteen artists recorded it, including Fess Parker himself, with a combined record sale of over four million copies.

Of course, Walt Disney wasn't alone in marketing Crockett merchandise. Even a powerful entity like Disney couldn't copyright an historical character; any toy manufacturer who so desired could churn out Crockett ephemera to their heart's content. It has been estimated that no fewer than 3,000 items bearing Crockett's name and likeness flooded the marketplace during the tumultuous months of the craze.

The Crockett craze represented an important moment in marketing history. For the first time, an entire generation of kids had discretionary income and knew what they wanted to buy with it. The craze was a defining moment for baby boomers, and its impact is still felt today, not only in our pop-culture memories but also in the way this and subsequent generations have chosen to view both Crockett and the Alamo. Like it or not, the long shadow of Fess Parker still touches the Alamo legacy, and will continue to, for the foreseeable future.

The avalanche of Crockett booty included the first-ever Alamo toys. Although the mission-fortress had inspired countless souvenirs, pictures, puzzles, books, and assorted trinkets over the previous century, the Crockett craze gave birth to the first toy Alamos, allowing children across America to turn an event of horror, bloodshed, mutilation, and death into hours of wholesome fun.

The Marx Alamo Playset

The first and most important toy in the world of Alamo collectibles is the Alamo playset, manufactured and distributed by the Louis Marx toy company. In one form or another, this enduring playset remained on the market for nearly two decades. Today, almost any version is highly

The first Marx "Davy Crockett at the Alamo" playset, released in 1955. Because it was rushed into production to capitalize on the "Crockett craze," Marx didn't have time to create Mexican soldiers, so Indians attacked the Alamo instead. From the author's collection.

prized by collectors and demands prices many, many times more than the original cost.

The Marx company was already well-known for its playsets, offering castles, ranch houses, and various forts, both historical and modern. The playsets consisted of metal buildings and outer walls, colorfully lithographed. The forts were both defended and attacked by plastic soldiers that came in sizes of 45mm, 54mm, or 60mm. The sets were filled out with plastic cannon, trees, and all kinds of accessories ranging from stoves, pumps, wells, and barrels to ladders, hitching posts, and lithographed tin flags.

Marx, like Disney, didn't anticipate the wave of enthusiasm for Crockett. The company rushed an official "Disney's Davy Crockett at the Alamo" playset into production in early 1955. Using new lithography, Marx adapted its "Fort Dearborn" building and walls into a beautiful, reasonably authentic Alamo. The Alamo church was in the familiar "shoebox" shape of many of the Marx buildings, and the humped gable attached to the top with folding tabs. For the Alamo purist who wanted a more authentic, humpless Alamo, this metal piece could also be detached.

The first "Davy Crockett at the Alamo" fort consisted of only the Alamo building and four walls, with no firing platforms. The fort was defended by the cavalry officers from the Fort Dearborn set. And, more distressingly for the historical-minded child, the Marx Alamo was attacked by Fort Dearborn Indians—the Marx company simply hadn't had time to complete the sculpting for its new Mexican soldiers. Probably very few kids minded, especially since the set was filled out with an official "Fess Parker as Davy Crockett" character figure, and an 8 x 10 photograph of Parker.

The follow-up playset, which arrived in stores a few months later, made up for the historical faux pas of the first. Now there were real Mexican soldiers in various poses of attack, although the Alamo was still defended by the Fort Dearborn cavalry. But in the revised playset, some of the Alamo's walls had firing platforms held on by plastic pegs, and there was a tin "1824" flag to wave stiffly above the besieged fortress. The Crockett character figure was still there, as was the 8 x 10 photograph. Now they were joined by a pamphlet that told the story of Davy Crockett and his last stand.

The Marx Alamo set continued to transform itself, year after year. Once the Crockett craze had died out, which happened rather abruptly in 1955, Marx dropped both Crockett and Disney from the equation, releasing a generic Alamo playset in 1960. There was also a bagged set called "Texas Frontier Fighters," which featured figures and horses from the Crockett set. Even the cream-colored Crockett figure was in the bag—but his base no longer identified him as Fess Parker. Interestingly, while Marx erased all mention of Disney or Crockett—or even the Alamo—from this bagged set, the artwork on the header card is clearly based on the "last stand" scene in the official Disney "Golden Book," *Davy Crockett, King of the Wild Frontier* (1955).

Various versions of the Marx Alamo playset remained in release at least through the seventies. The rarest of these was the "Border Battle" set—a miniature playset with an odd plastic Alamo defended by tiny hand-painted soldiers, in the same poses as those in the full-size playset.

The Ideal Toy Company also came out with an Alamo playset at about this time. Like the Marx version, the first Ideal set featured Indians and the second featured Mexican soldiers. Unlike the relative

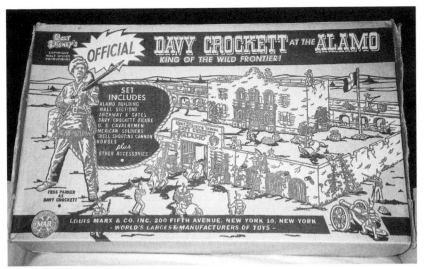

A later Marx "Davy Crockett at the Alamo" playset. This one included Mexican soldiers—and a lithographed metal "1824" flag. From the author's collection.

The Ideal Alamo playset. Not the last word in authenticity, but it was colorful and durable. From the author's collection.

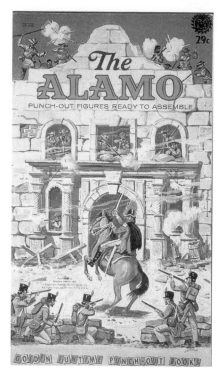

The Golden Funtime Alamo Punchout Book, released in 1960. From the author's collection.

authenticity and beautiful lithography of the Marx set, the Ideal Alamo was a highly stylized toy. The church façade was represented by a bright red piece of molded soft plastic, attached to two bendable lithographed metal walls. The 60mm figures were culled from various existing Ideal playsets, with the result that the Alamo had pioneers in coonskin caps fighting alongside Revolutionary War soldiers against a few Mexican soldiers wearing tall shakos.

A cheaper alternative to the Alamo playset also arrived in 1960, the same year that John Wayne's *The Alamo* was released to theaters. This was the Golden Funtime Punchout Book. In this colorful publication, figures, accessories, cannon—even the Alamo itself—could be punched from heavy cardboard pages to build an attractive, if rather insubstantial, fort. It wasn't exactly Marx quality, but at 25 cents, it made a good impulse purchase for the burgeoning Alamo scholar.

John Wayne's THE ALAMO Tie-ins

Oddly, while the Golden Funtime Punchout Book and the 1960 Marx Alamo playset appeared on the market at about the same time as John Wayne's epic film, the release of *The Alamo* was accompanied by virtually none of the usual marketing tie-ins. For example, while almost every John Wayne film of the period was accompanied by a comic book, there was no American *Alamo* comic. There were no games or puzzles—and only one toy. The only other collectibles were a few records, described later. Perhaps Wayne felt that the Crockett craze had already burnt out consumer interest in the subject five years earlier. It was almost certainly a tactical error that denied him and his film considerable additional income. Five years is a long time for children; an entire new generation had already sprung up between the Crockett craze and Wayne's *Alamo*.

But it isn't quite true that there were *no* tie-ins. One improbable toy was released in the United States—a pair of six-guns in holster—with a clear tie-in to Wayne's film on the packaging. Because there were obviously no six-guns in the film itself, it seems a peculiar choice, particularly since it's the *only* toy that was connected to *The Alamo* at all.

In France, two different *Alamo* comic books were released—but comic books of a very different kind than American kids were used to. Both were comprised not of cartoon art but of photographs from the film. Today, these books are highly prized among collectors, who can expect to spend well over $100 each to obtain them—if they can be found at all. But for fans of the Wayne film, until recently the books have had a different kind of value. Before the full-length 70mm version of *The Alamo* was discovered in Canada in 1990, these French comic books were the only access to the film's semi-legendary cut scenes that were presumed lost forever.

There were only three book tie-ins to the Wayne film, as opposed to the dozens—if not hundreds—that accompanied the Disney Crockett programs. A paperback version of Lon Tinkle's *Thirteen Days to Glory* (1958) was released with a still from *The Alamo* on the back but no further ties to the film. Avon books published Steve Frazee's novel *The Alamo* and represented it as a novelization of the *Alamo*'s script by James Edward Grant: "A thrilling book—now a magnificent movie—of one of the most dramatic events in America's history: 'Remember the Alamo!'" In fact (leaving aside the obvious quibble that the Alamo wasn't exactly an event in America's history), Frazee's book actually has no connection whatsoever to Wayne's film, except for the photographs on the front and back and inside the front cover. It's a surprisingly good book—one of the best Alamo novels, in fact—but its choice as the *Alamo* motion picture tie-in seems completely arbitrary.

Music lovers had a few more chances to acquire souvenirs of John Wayne's film. The soundtrack album featured highlights of the superb symphonic score by Dimitri Tiomkin, two dialogue excerpts spoken by John Wayne ("Republic. I like the sound of the word . . .") and performances by Marty Robbins and The Brothers Four. Tex Beneke, once a popular singer with the Glenn Miller Orchestra, recorded his own album, "Music from the Film 'The Alamo'" (RCA Camden), featuring some relatively authentic interpretations of Tiomkin's original score with a few interesting variations. And there were, of course, a few vocals by ol' Tex himself who, the liner notes tell us, "has been promoting Texas and the Big A for many years." The "Big A," we can only presume, is the Alamo.

Folk-music group The Easy Riders also contributed a tie-in to Wayne's *Alamo* with their LP "Remember the Alamo" on the Kapp label. The Easy Riders mixed some of the songs from the film, such as "Green Leaves of Summer" and "Ballad of the Alamo" with other "great songs of the Southwest in the days of the Alamo" such as "Green Grow the Lilacs" and "The Girl I Left Behind." Today, the album is more valuable for its cover than its music. It features a full-color shot of a battle scene from Wayne's movie. Oddly, the LP's art director chose a production still that shows Mexicans attacking the Alamo church, but no defenders defending it. Worse, just behind the fort you can clearly see a large yellow school bus and the cab of a semi truck. This is probably the shot that has led to persistent rumors about the school bus being visible in the film itself. It isn't.

"Ballad of the Alamo" was also released as a single by Marty Robbins, by a folk duo called Bud and Travis (no relation), and by a group called The Sons of Texas. The recording by The Sons of Texas is quite collectible today because of its excellent cover art. Golden Records released this single in both 45 and 78 rpm.

Undoubtedly the oddest recording of "Ballad of the Alamo" came in 1969, when the British pop group The Fortunes released it as a single. It's not known exactly why this group, best known for their Top 40 hit "You've Got Your Troubles, I've Got Mine," recorded this Western tune—already nearly a decade old. Even the band members themselves have no recollection as to who thought this would be a hit single for them. For the record, it wasn't.

Frankie Avalon recorded at least two extended-play records in Europe featuring songs from *The Alamo*. He also recorded a single of "Here's to the Ladies" for American release. Several artists recorded the haunting "Green Leaves of Summer," which was also nominated for an Academy Award. In 1988, the country group The Wagoneers released

Sheet music to "The Alamo Rag." The record version of this tune, released by Edison in 1910, might be the first Alamo song ever recorded. From the author's collection.

an album entitled *Stout and High*. The title song is a bouncy ode to the Alamo written by vocalist-guitarist Monte Warden. Its slight connection to Wayne's *The Alamo* comes at the beginning and the end of the song, when trumpeter Herb Alpert performs a solo version of the "Deguello" composed by Dimitri Tiomkin.

Other Alamo Recordings

However, the flurry of Alamo-related records and songs of the 1950s and 1960s did not represent the first recorded Alamo music. In 1910, Ben Deely and Percy Wenrich whipped up a lively ragtime number called "The Alamo Rag." This jaunty tune, which was recorded the same year on the Edison label, doesn't bother itself with patriotic themes or reverent odes to sacrifice; instead, it's all about fun. Here's the first verse:

> Way down South in San Antonio,
> That's the place they have the Alamo;
> That's the place they dance to pass
> The time away—
> both night and day, they do that sway.
>
> Place your arm around your lady's waist
> Just to show the folks you've got good taste
> Music starts a playing and away you go
> Oh oh, so slow—that's the Alamo!

(chorus) Oh—that Alamo Rag, that Alamo drag
Now honey if you think this talk is phoney
Take a trip to San Antony
Lawdy I could just die
Whenever they cry,
Play the Alamo Rag!

A far more serious Alamo recording was made in 1947. This was "The Alamo," a symphonic piece by Don Gillis (1912–1978), a Texan composer with over 150 works to his credit. Gillis, whose music ranged from classical to jazz to pop, always tried to fill his work with a uniquely American flavor. "The Alamo" sounds like the score to a movie that was never made—accessible, yet moving, flavored with passages that recall hymns or folk tunes. Sadly, Gillis's "The Alamo" never seems to have been recorded again after its original pressing in 1947. This fine piece, alternately exuberant and elegiac, deserves to be rediscovered by another generation of music—and Alamo—lovers.

The other Alamo music that followed was neither so serious nor so expressive. Except for motion picture scores, Alamo music almost always comes in the form of songs—often funny ones. In 1961, the DRT got into another of its customary uproars over the threat of pop culture. A new song, "Coward at the Alamo" by "Brother" Dave Gardner, found fun in the saga of Alamo deserter Moses Rose—even though Rose wasn't mentioned by name in the song.

Actually, it was only barely a song. Instead—not unlike Larry Verne's "Please Mr. Custer (I Don't Wanna Go)" from a year earlier— it was a comedy rant that dared poke fun at the heroes of a tragic, sacred event. Gardner's "Coward" is an 1836 hipster who talks like a beatnik:

Now listen man, I'm gonna split. I mean I'm vacating these premises. Now you all are either awful brave or you haven't looked over that wall lately, because there's a million mad Mescans out there, and they're gonna hit this adobe hacienda like a blue norther.

To further add insult to injury, Gardner's song placed both Davy Crockett ("that would make a swingin' TV series") *and* Daniel Boone in the Alamo. And he suggested that the entire battle was fought over all the tequila that the Texans hoarded inside the Alamo's walls.

Ironically, "Coward at the Alamo" was probably more popular in San Antonio than in the rest of the country. Most of the record stores in town quickly sold all of their copies of the record and had to reorder.

One Alamo hostess suggested that Gardner should be tarred and feathered. She said, "I think it is an outrage. Trying to tear down our heroes is subversive. It is the very thing the Communists try to do to our heroes and our institutions."[1]

Mrs. Edwin R. Simmang, chairman of the Alamo Committee for the DRT, threatened to ask the State Convention of the DRT to take some action against the song. "The Alamo," asserted Mrs. Simmang, "is nothing to joke about. The song doesn't tell the truth."[2]

Several other Alamo-related LPs were recorded in the 1950s and 1960s. Most of them were dramatized stories for children, complete with music, dialogue, and bombastic sound effects. Possibly the most effective of these was *Remember the Alamo* (Noble Records, 1960), which was narrated by the distinguished actor Claude Rains and featured a musical score by guitarist-composer Tony Mottola. The script, by Michael Avallone, is a tried-and-true, by-the-books Alamo, but told with simplicity and dignity.

Which is more than can be said for the "True Action Adventure Series" recording of *Remember the Alamo* seven years later. This double heaping of Alamo corn, which promises to "bring authentic realism into your home," has all of the Alamo defenders speaking in raspy cowboy voices, and a final battle sequence that causes the mind's eye to conjure a scene in which as many as a dozen men are quietly fighting. Neither the scriptwriter nor any of the actors are credited anywhere on the LP, possibly for fear of reprisals by irate consumers.

More Alamo Fun

Although the Louis Marx Company nearly had the market cornered on Alamo playsets, other companies have produced their own versions in recent years. Some of these are toys, but most are aimed at adult collectors with a taste for authentic dioramas and historical tableaux. BMC Toys released a low-cost Alamo playset that was designed by sculptor Tom Feeley, whose large and intricate Alamo diorama is a centerpiece at

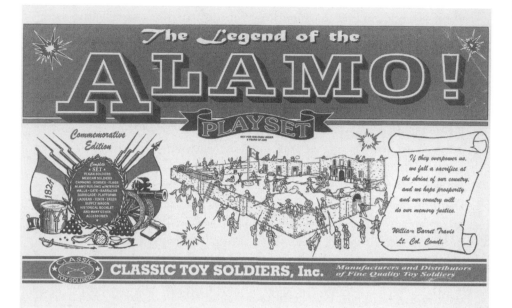

Craig R. Covner's art for the "Legend of the Alamo" playset, from Classic Toy Soldiers, Inc. Courtesy of Craig R. Covner.

Castle or Alamo? What's the difference? The instructions for "Border Battle," Marx's miniature Alamo playset. From the collection of Craig R. Covner.

The Crockett craze was reflected everywhere for a few heady months. This issue of *Little Lulu* is from 1956. From the author's collection.

the Alamo Museum/Gift Shop in San Antonio. This set featured a large-scale Alamo façade made of soft plastic, made to be proportionate with its 54mm soldiers. Unlike most Alamo toys, Feeley's Alamo church has no humped gable, nor the upper windows that were added by the U. S. Army in the late 1840s—it's the most authentic toy rendition of the Alamo's face. The figures of the Mexican army and the Alamo defenders were also released separately in a bagged set, along with a cardboard Alamo that serves as both toy and toy box.

A far more elaborate Alamo playset arrived in the late 1990s, made by Classic Toy Soldier Company. It featured a lithographed metal fort like the Marx set but went to greater pains to replicate the full Alamo compound of 1836. For the first time in toy history, an Alamo playset came complete with south-wall gate, two-story long barracks, cannon ramps, and other interesting accessories. The playset's Alamo church, however, is a frustrating one for the purist—it is neither the humped façade of the modern Alamo nor the flat-topped building of 1836, but a kind of compromise between the two. But it does have a removable back, which allows the collector to fill the side rooms with powder kegs, or to place Jim Bowie on his sickbed inside the church.

Despite the disappointment of the Alamo chapel, the CTS playset is an impressive achievement. With its beautifully sculpted soldiers in a satisfying variety of colors and poses, and its beautifully detailed silk screening—designed by Alamo authority Craig R. Covner—the CTS "Legend of the Alamo" is a remarkable and valuable playset, as much historical diorama as toy.

For the more serious (and patient) Alamo buff, several cardboard-cutout Alamo models were produced. The cover to Mark Wheatley's 1982 "Build the Alamo" promises "a great family project ready for easy assembly" and pictures a happy father (dressed as a Mexican officer) and son (dressed like Davy Crockett) putting the finishing touches on the cardboard version of the modern-day Alamo chapel. But that dream of easy assembly is quickly shattered when one actually tries to assemble the thing. Model builders with a steady hand and a keen eye for detail might do a great job with it; but others—certain writers, for instance—will end up with something that resembles a de Kooning collage.

In 1968, Monte Enterprises published an even more complex cardboard model. This one replicated the entire mission compound of

Left: The Alamo pinball game (ca. 1931). From the author's collection.

Above: The Alamo pinball game (detail). From the author's collection.

1836—complete with roofless, but nonetheless humped, church. Each inch of the model equals ten feet of the real thing. Once constructed correctly, this makes a large and impressive diorama; but constructing it correctly . . . there's the rub.

The popular Give-a-Show projector appeared in the 1950s. A toy version of a magic lantern, the Give-a-Show was a handheld, battery-powered plastic projector—a kind of glorified flashlight—through which was pushed a strip of seven 35mm color slides. There were many editions of the Give-a-Show projector over the years; most of them featured slides of cartoon characters such as the Flintstones or Yogi Bear. But in 1962 a special "Adventure Time" edition was released. This box included sixteen true stories about everything from the first monkey in space, to the story of the Wright Brothers, to the saga of Hannibal crossing the Alps. And, it told the story of the Alamo—titled "182 Brave Men."

The "Adventure Time" Give-a-Show also came with two 45-rpm records, featuring narration, music, and sound effects. A helpful bell sounded whenever it was time to advance the filmstrip to the next slide. With just seven slides, the Alamo story was told in only the simplest terms; but the sound, excellent color artwork—and the participation of the "projectionist"—combined to make it a memorable little Alamo movie.

Another slideshow version of the Alamo had appeared back in 1955, when Walt Disney Productions authorized a series of Tru-Vu slides based on the Davy Crockett series. Tru-Vu slides were similar to the more popular Viewmaster slides, except that these images were placed on a rectangular card instead of a wheel. But, like Viewmasters, the Tru-Vu slides were double-printed to give the illusion of three dimensions.

Interestingly, the Tru-Vu Crockett slides were not taken during the production of the shows themselves. Fess Parker and Buddy Ebsen were brought back and posed in an entirely new set with different actors. For kids who had virtually memorized the original "At the Alamo" episode, the change must have been curious, at least. Today, the different images give these slides additional value, since they don't simply repeat familiar images from the show.

Board Games and Jigsaw Puzzles

Board game aficionados also had an opportunity to fight the battle of the Alamo. "Davy Crockett's Alamo Game," published by Lowell Toy Mfg. Corp. in 1955, was a kind of Trivial Alamo Pursuit. The object of the game was to fill all the spaces on your ALAMO card by answering questions such as "What is the Deguelo [sic]?" "When was Davy Crockett Born?" and "Who was the first American to lead the settlers into Texas?" The first player to fill his card had to call out "Alamo!" to win.

In 1966, the Solodar Company in San Antonio released the "Battle of the Alamo Game," which invited players to "Join the heroes of the Alamo and change the course of history if you can . . ." The game came with four sets of rules for playing at various levels of difficulty; however, at any level the game seemed dauntingly complex. One player was to take command of the Alamo and direct his men there. All the other players were Santa Anna's army, trying to get over the wall. The rulebook says:

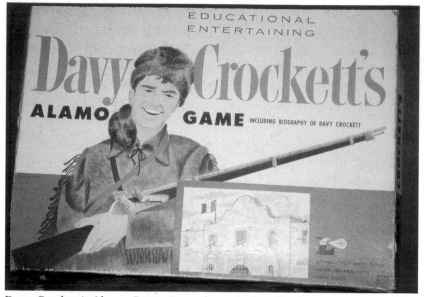

Davy Crockett's Alamo Game. From the author's collection.

The Alamo Defenders "fire" the cannons from time to time and "hit" Enemy soldiers who are waiting to go over the walls. As Enemy Soldiers break through the Barricades they are engaged in hand-to-hand combat with the Defenders. Near the end of the game the pace changes and there is the final storming of the walls, corresponding to the last stand, on the thirteenth day, at the Alamo.

The directions also promise that, "contrary to history, the Defenders of the Alamo can win this game." To help things along, the game comes with a booklet telling the Alamo story, a letter from the game's designer David Solodar, and an illustrated booklet of the rules. There was also a "courtesy certificate" that, if filled out and mailed, could bring in return "free bulletins about the 'Battle of the Alamo' game when they are printed."

Those Alamo-philes of a more contemplative turn of mind might prefer working on one of the several Alamo jigsaw puzzles. These started appearing at least as far back as the 1920s and, with almost no exceptions, are made up of modern-day photographs. These were sometimes

An Alamo jigsaw puzzle from the 1940s.
From the author's collection.

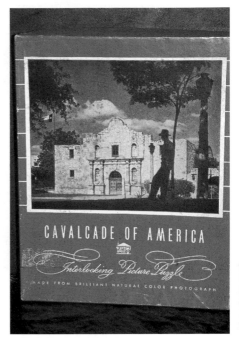

hand-colored but more often, as in Playtime House's "Cavalcade of America" Alamo puzzle of 1944, were "made from brilliant natural color photography."

At least two Alamo jigsaw puzzles depicted historical scenes. In 1969 the Humble Oil & Refining Company released a series of historical paintings-as-puzzles packaged in, for some reason, sealed tin cans. The series was called "Great Moments in American History" and included twelve subjects from "Columbus Sails On" (Number One) to "John Glenn Orbits the Earth (Number Twelve). "The Battle of the Alamo," Number Nine in the series, depicted a heroic group of men at a cannon that is in the process of being fired. One man holds a torch aloft, another defiantly waves a large 1824 flag, and in the background stands a relatively authentic Alamo church—without the usual anachronistic hump.

Perhaps the rarest Alamo jigsaw puzzle is that released by Edu-Cards in cooperation with Landmark Books. Each of these historical themed puzzles—which featured, in addition to the Alamo, the Vikings, the Constitution, and the Santa Fe Trail—utilized the artwork from Landmark's series of children's books on those subjects. The vivid Alamo painting showed bearded defenders in beaded buckskins fighting off Mexican soldiers in front of a modern-day Alamo. By the time the puzzle was released in 1962, the picture, painted by Taylor Oughton, would already have been quite familiar to any child who had read Robert Penn Warren's wonderful *Remember the Alamo* (1958), otherwise illustrated by William Moyers.

The most recent Alamo jigsaw puzzle, as of this writing, is based on Richard Luce's 1997 painting, "For God and Texas." This battle scene takes a fairly standard viewpoint—at the wooden palisade in front of

Classic Toys Soldiers' metal Alamo church from the "Legend of the Alamo" playset. From the author's collection.

the church. It's a lively and well-executed painting that isn't quite as compelling historically as it might be; it is so clearly modeled on the John Wayne set in Brackettville, and the Alamo defenders are based pretty obviously on modern-day reenactors. To be fair, though, the other Alamo jigsaw puzzles aren't all that authentic themselves—so why start now?

In fact, virtually none of the puzzles, board games, slideshows, songs, playsets, and toy soldiers even pretend to accurately portray the actual historical moment of March 6, 1836. And why should they? They are meant only for fun. The defenders of the Alamo and the brave men who attacked the fort would, no doubt, find it peculiar in the extreme that their day of terror, pain, and death has been translated into so many lighthearted moments of play. But on reflection, perhaps they wouldn't mind; these toys and games have engaged—and continue to engage—the imaginations of children and adults. And through the fun they plant a seed—helping to ensure that forever after, those who play with them will always remember the Alamo.

Rebuilding the Alamo

In 1938, as two world's fairs were in the planning stages, it was announced that the Texas state buildings at each fair would be patterned after the Alamo. In the *Houston Chronicle*, Mary Wittliff reported the details of the proposed Alamo replicas for both the 1939 New York World's Fair and the 1939 San Francisco Golden Gate Exposition, but she allowed herself to wonder if the Alamo was just the right building for such a signal honor:

> The Alamo as it now stands in San Antonio is a rather plain
> building, and its impressiveness lies mainly in the story connected
> with it. The realization that inside those gray stone walls 185
> men deliberately and unflinchingly sacrificed themselves in order
> that "Texas might be free" is one of the most awe-inspiring
> records of history.

Leaving aside the obvious rebuttals that the walls are cream-colored, not gray, that few Alamo defenders actually died inside the church anyway, and that there was undoubtedly plenty of flinching going on in the predawn hours of March 6, Wittliff's characterization of the Alamo as "a rather plain building" is simply beyond the pale. Indeed, the simple carved beauty of the Alamo, with its slightly flawed symmetry, has inspired artists and sculptors for well over a century and a half. Besides, the Alamo has also cast its spell over any number of people who have been led to replicate the old mission church for houses and businesses, and sometimes just as a kind of tribute. Certainly what happened at the Alamo has inspired many, if not most, of the replicas.

But the alluring and timeless beauty of the building is also a factor.

At any rate, the two world's fair buildings were only *inspired* by the Alamo—they weren't actual replicas. The San Antonio architectural design firm, Adams and Adams, was commissioned to "execute these buildings to resemble the Alamo as closely as possible in consideration of the demands of fair grounds," wrote Mary Wittliff in the *Houston Post*. However, she added, "the interior will be more brightly decorated" with "high backed and carved chairs, Spanish shawls, Mexican rugs, pottery, brilliantly colored floors and wrought iron lamps."[1]

The Texas state building from the 1915 Panama-Pacific International Exposition in San Francisco had also been heavily inspired by the Alamo, although it came off as a kind of hodgepodge of several Texas mission styles. Its façade was very clearly patterned after the Alamo, but in back of its humped gable was a red-tiled, peaked roof. On the right side of the building rose a bell tower, highly reminiscent of the one at San Antonio's Mission San Jose.

In fact, this Texas state building very much resembles another Alamo replica, one that is still standing in San Antonio. The Catholic church called San Antonio de Padua, dedicated in 1936, also boasts a bell tower, painted a brilliant white. Otherwise, it is the spitting image of the Alamo—and it was intended to be. An historical marker to the side of the church proclaims it the National Shrine of St. Anthony or the "New Alamo" built to commemorate "the 200th anniversary (March 1731) of the founding of San Antonio, the 700th anniversary of the death of St. Anthony (June 13, 1231) and the Centenary of the Fall of the Alamo (March 6, 1836)."

Other Alamos

The idea of creating replicas of the Alamo is not a new one, but it is sometimes a controversial one. When plans were announced to build another Alamo for the 1936 Dallas Central Centennial Exposition, the Daughters of the Republic of Texas (custodians of the Alamo) and the San Antonio Centennial Association protested immediately. They felt that if the thousands of visitors who would attend the fair got the full Alamo experience in Dallas, then there would be no reason for them to come to San Antonio to visit the real thing. Indeed, people might think that the Dallas Alamo was the real thing.

The Texas State Building from the 1915 Panama-Pacific International Exposition, San Francisco. From the collection of Craig R. Covner.

[An] exact replica of the Alamo would cause confusion among visitors to the exposition as to where the Alamo is located. School children, for instance, are likely to think that the replica is the actual Alamo and the key fight of Texas independence was fought in Dallas.[2]

The Centennial Association planned to protest the building of such a replica, "even if court action is necessary."[3]

Further, "association members charged that engineers for the exposition scaled the Alamo court yards on a Sunday to take measurements of the historic shrine. This led to the belief a duplicate of the Alamo was to be built in Dallas."[4] Planning to build a counterfeit Alamo was one thing; crawling all over the shrine with measuring devices was quite another.

However, once the DRT and the Centennial Association were assured that the Alamo replica would be only half the size of the real Alamo—and clearly labeled as a copy on a plaque to be attached to the front of the building—they agreed to call off their lawsuit.

A newspaper article on the controversy, with the headline "Alamo Replica Storm Calmed," ended this way:

It was announced in Dallas Thursday that exposition officials planned to reconstruct a small replica of the Alamo which has stood on the fairgrounds many years. Recently it was razed to make room for other buildings. It will be located at a new location, it was said.[5]

This little postscript clarifies exactly why the San Antonio Centennial Association had gotten so bent out of shape over the prospect of a new Alamo replica: professional jealousy. The one that had stood in Dallas since 1909 had proved to be an enormously popular spot with tourists and school groups. In fact, an undated newspaper article claimed, "The replica of the Alamo at Fair Park attracts more visitors each year than the original Alamo at San Antonio, according to J. B. Martin, in charge of the building during the State Fair." The ersatz Alamo had been visited by people from all over the world, as well as by "relatives of Travis, Crockett, and other Texas heroes."

This half-sized Alamo had been built at the behest of George B. Dealey, vice president and general manager of the *Dallas News*. In June 1909, Dealey sent J. P. Hubbell of the architectural firm Hubbell and Greene to San Antonio to gather data. For three days, Hubbell not only measured every architectural element of the building, but he even measured "the broken places in that time-worn stone and the location of the cannon shot in the ancient walls."[6]

Hubbell was followed to San Antonio by a Mr. Wood of the Alex Watson Construction Company. Wood took photographs of the carvings and all other details. Further, watercolor paintings were produced so that the replica would perfectly reflect the color of the original.

Builders worked on the tiny Alamo for two months. Their last task was to meticulously "ruin" the walls, "producing a reproduction so natural as to startle those familiar with the venerated old mission chapel, especially as trained hands artfully discolored the walls so that it might seem the work of the ages."[7]

Inside, the old wooden rafters (since removed) and the ancient iron lamps were recreated perfectly; the lamps were even "artfully rusted." Then the interior was decorated with a reproduction of Theodore Gentilz's painting, "The Fall of the Alamo," and two framed poems: "The Alamo" by Alvan E. Farr and "Crockett in the Alamo" by Amy

The remarkable Alamo built for the Errol Flynn western *San Antonio* (1945). From the author's collection.

Pearl Cosby. Adina de Zavala, then president of the DRT, contributed pictures of many of the Alamo heroes, as well as a portrait of "Ven. Anthony Margil, the Francisan missionary, founder of the Alamo and other Texas missions."[8]

In his dedication speech, Dealey said:

> We all believe in rearing monuments to our departed heroes to keep us reminded of glorious deeds, and the older a country becomes, the more attention is given to such acts. But for the heroes of the Alamo, no monument, be it ever so grand, can equal that furnished by the historic walls themselves, and it devolves upon every loyal son of Texas to see those walls preserved intact, that those sacred stones, baptized in the blood of splendid heroes, may, until they crumble into dust, remain mute reminders of that immortal struggle.

Unfortunately, San Antonio is so far removed from the great mass of our people that it is probable that not more than one-

San Antonio de Padua, the "new Alamo" in San Antonio, Texas. From the collection of Craig R. Covner.

third of our four million population ever have or ever will see the dearest spot to the Texan heart.[9]

It is, perhaps, similar reasoning that has led to the construction of at least a dozen Alamo replicas that currently stand at various places around Texas. It's a big state; why shouldn't every Texan have greater access to the Alamo?

There is a miniature Alamo in Maxey Park in Pecos, a chiropractic office that looks like the Alamo near Tyler, and a veterinary clinic/Alamo replica in Odessa. The building housing the corporate offices of Kwik-Kopy in Houston is built to look like the Alamo. And this one, for some reason, sparked a mild rebuke from the DRT: "There is only one Alamo as far as we're concerned," said Peggy Dibrell, Secretary for the Committee of the DRT.[10]

Ken Freeman, of Holiday Lakes, Texas, lives in an Alamo replica he built himself. "It took us eight months," he told a reporter. I made my own blueprints. It's as close as I could get from reading articles in *Texas Highways* magazines." Freeman said that the "wildest thing about building this was the columns. I couldn't buy them, so I built them myself using flower pot molds and molds from an ice cream maker."[11]

Javier Nava had the columns on *his* Alamo in El Paso hand-carved. But then, he spent nearly a million dollars on the Alamo Ballroom and Convention Center. The website www.navaenterprises.com explains how they did it:

> We at Nava Enterprises, Inc. have fought our own battle to bring a part of the Alamo history to El Paso. Several trips to San Antonio and long hours of research were necessary to accomplish our mission. Blueprints were provided by the Daughters of the Republic of Texas, to ensure authenticity. The stone for the building facade and the entry floor is the same type used in the original. One hundred and twenty tons were shipped in from a quarry 10 miles from the Alamo in San Antonio. The stone, the columns and the decorative stones were hand carved and installed by rock masons who have done restoration on the original Alamo.

Nava's Alamo includes an auditorium and dance hall. It is normally used for weddings and *quinceanera* (fifteenth birthday) celebrations, but

The Alamo replica built for the 1936 Dallas Central Centennial Exposition. From the author's collection.

Nava also likes to show Alamo movies there and sometimes presents live Alamo dramas.

Another interesting Alamo replica, and a slightly more impressionistic one, stands in Brackenridge Park near Hildebrand Avenue in San Antonio. Built in the early twenties by then Parks Commissioner Ray Lambert, it was originally intended to be used as a hay barn for the zoo. In 1956, Parks Director Robert Frazer spent $4,500 remodeling it as an office building, and it now serves as one of the headquarters for San Antonio Parks and Recreation.[12] Built of dark stone, the parks building is clearly inspired by the Alamo without attempting to duplicate it precisely. There is a squared tower on one side and, with a nod to the other San Antonio missions, a replica of Mission San Jose's famous "rose window" on the front.

Several faux Alamo facades currently dot the Texas landscape. Caterer Don Strange keeps one for a party backdrop at his ranch near San Antonio. The Houston club City Streets also houses a nearly full-size Alamo façade. The San Antonio Chamber of Commerce has a traveling Alamo façade made of polystyrene and fiberglass. The structure, which measures twenty-two feet by forty-eight feet, is used at conventions, trade shows, and other events.

But not all Alamo replicas are in Texas. You can still—barely—see one unusual example at 522 E. Broadway in San Gabriel, California.

The little Alamo, built on the State Fairgrounds in Dallas in 1909. From the author's collection.

Kwik-Kopy Headquarters in Cypress, Texas. Courtesy of International Center for Entrepreneurial Development, Inc.

The Alamo Ballroom and Convention Center in El Paso, Texas. Courtesy of Javier Nava.

San Antonio Parks and Recreation Offices, Brackenridge Park, San Antonio, Texas. Photograph by Claire McCulloch Thompson.

Originally built as the San Gabriel Wedding Gardens, the building is now virtually hidden behind an apartment building that was built close enough that you can touch both buildings at the same time. No one at the San Gabriel historical society seems to be very clear on why the building was made to resemble the Alamo or, indeed, who built it. The best they could remember was that it was the brainchild of a "Mr. Martin."

Another oddball Alamo replica stands a few miles away, on the back lot of Universal Studios. The façade was originally constructed in the early eighties for the comedy-mystery *Cloak and Dagger*, starring Henry Thomas. Some scenes for this San Antonio–based movie were shot at the real Alamo; but the door, columns, and icon niches were reproduced at the studio for close-up scenes. The Universal Alamo has shown up in the background of various productions, from the opening "silent movie" scenes in the comedy *Three Amigos!* (1986) to Enrique Iglesias's music video for his song "Bailamos" (1999). In fact, it has appeared as the Alamo in only one other instance—in Steven Spielberg's *Amazing Stories* episode, "Alamo Jobe" (1986). In that fantasy, the partial façade was augmented by a matte painting to make one very peculiar-looking

Alamo façade used by the San Antonio Visitors and Convention Center. Courtesy of San Antonio Visitors and Convention Center.

The former San Gabriel Wedding Gardens in San Gabriel, California. This Alamo replica is obscured by an apartment building that was constructed only inches away. Photograph by Claire McCulloch Thompson.

Alamo. Even without the matte painting, the façade looks pretty strange when seen today on Universal's "Mexican Village" set. For some reason, someone recently topped the little structure with a "hump" gable, just like the real Alamo. But because the replica isn't full-scale—or even the full building—the hump sits atop it like an ill-fitting hat.

A far more authentic Alamo was constructed for the Errol Flynn western, *San Antonio* (1945). Faithfully copied by Warner Bros. art directors, this Alamo is unique among motion picture replicas in that it is attached to the long barracks adorned in their U. S. army additions of the 1840s and

The interior of the *San Antonio* Alamo (1945). From the collection of Paul Andrew Hutton.

A remarkably convincing view of Alamo Plaza in the 1870s, from the Errol Flynn film, *San Antonio* (1945). From the collection of Paul Andrew Hutton.

A beautiful Alamo set constructed for the 1915 epic, *Martyrs of the Alamo*. From the author's collection.

Art director Al Ybarra constructing the set for John Wayne's *The Alamo* (1960). From the author's collection.

1850s. The effect is breathtakingly believable, but the *San Antonio* Alamo indulges in a slight anachronism for poetic and dramatic purposes. While the Alamo façade already shows the upper windows and "hump" of the army redesign, the interior is still roofless and ruined— all the better for a terrifically moody, moonlit gunfight at the film's climax. Sadly, this marvelous Alamo was never used in another film.

Alamo Village

Certainly, the most elaborate Alamo replica of them all does indeed stand in Texas, and has been visited by tens of thousands of pilgrims over the years. It is Happy Shahan's "Alamo Village," the set built on Shahan's 22,000-acre ranch near Brackettville for the filming of John Wayne's *The Alamo* (1960).

Art director Al Ybarra designed Wayne's Alamo. Wayne wanted to construct the entire mission compound not as false fronts as are usually built for movies, but as full, three-dimensional buildings. Publicity for the film claimed that Ybarra went to Spain to consult the original plans

The completed church as seen in John Wayne's *The Alamo*.

The Waynamo as it appeared in the early 1980s, during production of Jesus Trevino's *Seguin* (1982). From the collection of Paul Andrew Hutton.

Interior of the church in 1988, after being rebuilt for the IMAX production *Alamo . . . the Price of Freedom.* Photographed by the author.

Chapel Mission Park, San Antonio, Texas. From the author's collection.

for Mission San Antonio de Valero, and that the replica was built with meticulous regard to those plans.

Which, of course, is hogwash on several levels. There are no surviving plans of the original mission. And, while there are a couple of more-or-less contemporary plans of the fortified Alamo, circa 1836, it doesn't seem that Ybarra consulted them, either. The result is an impressive structure that is generally very convincing—certainly the most convincing movie Alamo. But Ybarra added visual flourishes that were all his own. The main gate on the south side of the Alamo was, according to all surviving description, a flat building. Ybarra gave it a graceful rise in the middle, and subtly shaded the area around the door with blue in a shape that suspiciously resembles the "A" as it appears in nearly all the publicity for the film.

Ybarra also elected to place stairs and a porch on the two-story portion of the long barracks closest to the church. There's no indication that such a porch existed during the siege, but it has its purposes in the film. As Brian Huberman and Ed Hugetz so perceptively noted, Travis (Laurence Harvey) is almost always in an elevated position in the film, always talking down at his men, either from horseback, from the top of the church, or from the steps that lead up to his headquarters in the long

Two Alamo Plaza Motor Courts. From the collection of Paul Andrew Hutton.

A movie theater in Los Angeles, California. Photo by Ned Huthmacher.

barracks.[13] So, from a dramatic point of view, this slight historical inaccuracy makes sense.

The same can be said for Ybarra's misplacement of San Antonio. Instead of placing it to the west of the Alamo, Ybarra had his crew build "San Antonio" directly to the south. But again, this was a deliberate choice, not made out of ignorance but as a way of best serving the film. The most photogenic angle of the Alamo in this film is from the south; the low barracks and gate leading to the wooden palisade form a beautiful frame for the church, seen in a three-quarters angle. Because the camera most often looked at the Alamo from that direction, the town as backdrop had to be exactly opposite. If San Antonio were in the "correct" place, there would be no real dimension to the space outside the Alamo. It isn't history; but compositionally, it's right.

The Alamo church has been compromised for similar reasons. Ybarra gave it the ruined gable, but couldn't resist giving it a slight rise in the middle, to suggest the hump. He also gave it the upper windows that weren't actually put there until 1850. The ornate carving around the door was partially replaced by plain stone slabs in the same 1850 remodeling, and Ybarra's version also contains this anachronism. And, although the real Alamo is constructed entirely of limestone, only the façade of Ybarra's is made that way. The interior is adobe and stucco.

Numerous films have been made on the Wayne set—fondly called the Waynamo by most buffs—and not all of them had to do with the

Alamo. The trouble is that every change made for a different kind of movie inevitably stayed in the picture when the next Alamo film came around. Hence, the hideous stone well built for *Bandolero* (1968) is there for Travis (Alec Baldwin) to stand on, hoping to give the Mexicans a better target in *The Alamo: 13 Days to Glory* (1987). The lumbering arches beside the church, constructed for *Barbarosa* (1982), have intruded on every Alamo film since. And the ornate portico added to the long barracks to make them look like a fancy hotel in *Rio Diablo* (1993) is still there, defended by Travis, Bowie, and Crockett in the abysmal *James A. Michener's "Texas"* (1994).

When the IMAX film *Alamo . . . the Price of Freedom* was filmed at Alamo Village in the summer of 1987, it was decided to make the set as accurate as possible. However, there was still Happy Shahan to contend with. Shahan was one shrewd businessman, and he wouldn't agree to anything that would damage the set. So, although the set designers wanted to level off the minor "hump" on the façade and fill in the anachronistic upper windows, Shahan would agree to no destruction whatsoever. The compromise was to fill in the upper windows and build a slight rise to the façade of the church to compensate for it. The result was, in its way, no more realistic than Ybarra's original. In some ways it looks *less* like the Alamo of 1836 than the design it replaced. The limestone had also darkened substantially over the years. Instead of cleaning it, to give it the cream color of the original—and of the real Alamo—the set designers darkened the surrounding walls instead. The result was that the walls resembled not limestone or adobe and stucco, but camouflage.

Years later, *Two for Texas* (1998) went into production. Although the film contained a single scene in the aftermath of the Alamo battle, it was decided not to go to Brackettville, but to create a new Alamo façade and film other scenes at San Antonio's Mission Espada. So for the first time in decades, an art director had the chance to create a façade that looked precisely like the Alamo did in 1836. At last, an Alamo movie would be made in which—for the only time in history—the façade of the Alamo would look not like the Ybarra recreation or some other bizarre variation on the Alamo, but like the real thing.

So, the art directors of *Two for Texas* got to work—and replicated the Waynamo. When they start making replicas of replicas, you know things have gone too far.

Alamo Ghosts

The fall of the Alamo has inspired many legends over the past century and a half. Most, of course, have been of a heroic or patriotic nature; the Alamo has entered the consciousness of the world as a place and an event of sacrifice and nobility, of pure-blooded ideals and unwavering resolve.

But the Alamo inspired other kinds of legends, too. It isn't at all surprising that this place which has seen so much horror and death, whose walls have been christened with both tears and blood, should now and again conjure up ghostly echoes of its past. For many San Antonians, the Alamo in the aftermath of its traumatic battle was a gloomy, if not downright spooky, place. In 1905, an unidentified citizen remembered his boyhood, playing in the ruined compound:

> When I first saw the Alamo, in 1845, it looked as it did at the time of the memorable siege. Not a stone had seemingly been disturbed. The bloodstains were visible on the walls. It was a veritable ruin, partly from the destruction caused by battle, but mostly from its long abandonment as the abode of man. No doors or windows shut out the sunshine or storm; millions of bats inhabited the crevices in the walls and flat dirt roofs, and in the twilight would pour forth in myriads. It was a meeting place for owls . . .[1]

Another writer described the Alamo as a "silent monument, grim, gloomy and peculiar, of all the horrors that were ever committed there."[2]

This fanciful version of the first Alamo ghost story by artist and Alamo afi-
cionado Michael Boldt takes a few liberties with the tale as passed along by
Adina de Zavala. Whereas de Zavala's ghosts with flaming swords merely
chased away the Mexicans attempting to tear down the Alamo, Boldt's ghosts
are mounted and deadly. Artwork courtesy of Michael Boldt.

A ruined, bloodstained old structure, darkened by swarms of bats, is
the kind of place liable to kindle the imagination. Sure enough, in the
years since, many witnesses have reported seeing wispy visions, hearing
muffled footsteps, and experiencing cold spots at various places around
the Alamo grounds. It is said ghosts are spirits that are bound to a certain place because of excessive trauma or because death was sudden and
the life it ended was unresolved. Others say that ghostly manifestations
are a kind of psychic movie—simply an endless replaying of some terrible or important moment, an event so powerful, so electric that it never
quite manages to dissipate from the atmosphere. Certainly, the Alamo
would easily qualify for ghost status under either of those definitions.
Perhaps the real surprise is that there aren't more Alamo ghost stories
than those already being told.

Poets and playwrights have frequently populated the place with wandering spirits. Ramsey Yelvington's *A Cloud of Witnesses* (1954) is a play about Alamo ghosts who return to the scene to discover if their sacrifice had been worthwhile. In "Alamo Jobe," an episode of Steven Spielberg's fantasy omnibus television series *Amazing Stories* (1986), a young Alamo defender steps directly from the battle into modern-day San Antonio. There, he finds a future filled with trite dialogue and pointless story lines. Jobe isn't a ghost exactly, but the situation is supernatural, as well as dull.

Around the turn of the last century, in the *New York Tribune,* writer Grantland Rice penned an excellent poem about a gathering of spirits at the Alamo. It's worth reprinting here, not only because the poem is a fine ghost tale in and of itself, but because of its obvious influence on later Alamo songs, such as "The Ballad of the Alamo" (1960) by Dimitri Tiomkin and Paul Francis Webster.

Ghosts of the Alamo

There's the tramp of a ghost on the low winds tonight,
    An echo that drifts like a dream on its way;
There's the blue of the specter that leaves for the fight,
    Grave-risen at last from a long vanished day;
There's the shout and the call of grim soul unto soul
As they rise one by one, out of death's shadowed glen
    To follow the bugle—the drum's muffled roll
    Where the Ghosts of the Alamo gather again.

I hear Crockett's voice as he leaps from the dust
    And waits at the call for an answering hail;
    And Bowie caresses a blade red with rust
    As deep in the shadows he turns to the trail;
    Still lost in the darkness that covers their sleep
    Their bodies may rest in a sand-mounded den,
But their spirits have come from the red, starry steep
    Where Ghosts of the Alamo gather again.

You think they've forgotten—because they have slept—
    The day Santa Anna charged in with his slaves;

Where five thousand men 'gainst a few hundred swept
And stormed the last rampart that stood for their graves?
   You think they've forgotten; but faint, from afar,
   Brave Travis is calling the roll of his men
And a voice answers "Here!" Through the shadows that bar
   Where Ghosts of the Alamo gather again.

There's a flash on a blade—and you thought it a star?
There's a light on the plain—and you thought it the moon?
You thought the wind echoed that anthem of war?
   Not knowing the lilt of an old border tune;
Gray shade after shade, stirred again unto breath;
Gray phantom by phantom they charge down the glen,
Where souls hold a hate that is greater than death,
   Where Ghosts of the Alamo gather again.

★ ★ ★

Ghosts are often said to touch the living with an icy hand, but the very first Alamo ghost legend was all about fire, not ice. In her book, *History and Legends of the Alamo and other Missions in and around San Antonio,* Adina de Zavala recounted a fantastic cautionary folk tale that dates to the days just after San Jacinto. General Andrade, who commanded 1,001 men in San Antonio, had been left to refortify the Alamo. For sixty-five days, Andrade's men worked at turning the battle-scarred compound back into a stronghold. But after Santa Anna's defeat at San Jacinto, General Andrade received orders on May 19, 1836 to undo everything he had just accomplished—he was to tear down the Alamo, spike the cannon, toss all the ammunition into the river, and generally render the place uninhabitable and undefendable. His men did as they were told and tore down most of the surrounding walls. They left standing the church, the long barracks, the south-wall gate and low barracks, and a few random smaller buildings.

According to the folk tale, there was an excellent reason Andrade's men left the job unfinished. Everywhere they turned, it was said, they were met by spirits wielding "flaming swords." As de Zavala tells it, these angry ghosts barred [the soldiers'] progress and soon frightened them off; that almost as fast as new relays of men were sent with orders to destroy the walls, they were overcome by fright; nor could threats or punishment induce them to return. They were permitted by the ghosts for a space to disarm the batteries, but the moment the walls of the buildings were threatened, there was the flaming sword in ghostly hands.[3]

According to de Zavala, the spirits did more than just threateningly wave their swords around. They also called out, "Depart, touch not these walls! He who desecrates these walls shall meet a horrible Fate! Multiplied afflictions shall seize upon him and a horrible and agonizing and avenging torture shall be his death!"[4] which would discourage most people. No doubt Ms. de Zavala wrote these words with a tinge of regret, perhaps wishing those sword-hauling spooks had shown up again in 1905 or so to help her run Clara Driscoll off during the "Second Battle of the Alamo."

Adina de Zavala ends her tale with a cryptic coda:

Search into the miserable lives and deaths of those responsible for the tearing down of part of the Alamo . . . is it not, at least, a strange coincidence that the man who, more than any other one person, was deliberately responsible for the destruction of the upper story of the old Alamo Fortress met such a horrible, agonizing fate?—entombed alive and consumed by flames—that his worst enemy could not fail to be moved with pity.[5]

But of whom she is speaking, she never makes clear. Andrade didn't die in such a terrible manner. Nor did Lt. Gov. Will Mayes, who gave the order in 1913 to tear down what was left of the upper story of the long barracks. (See Chapter Four for a more thorough, though substantially less supernatural, discussion of this event.)

The angry spirits with their fiery swords never reappeared, but it doesn't mean that paranormal activity at the Alamo ceased. In 1866 the city of San Antonio decided to tear down the "Galera," one of the few structures on the Alamo property remaining from the time of the battle in 1836. The Galera consisted of the main gate on the south side of the mission compound, and the rooms that joined it on either end. Most his-

The Galera, or south-wall gate building, was the site of a celebrated haunting when it was torn down in 1871. Guests in the Menger Hotel (which is said to have its own ghosts, thank you) saw "spectral forms" marching about in protest. From the author's collection.

torians believe that Jim Bowie died in one of these rooms. In the ensuing thirty years the Galera had been used as a jail, but it had fallen into such disrepair that it was thought best to raze it. But the Catholic Church objected and halted the demolition. However, even then the historic structure wasn't saved; it simply continued to deteriorate for five more years, until the city finally purchased it back from the church and knocked the Galera to the ground.

But according to legend, the Catholic Church didn't lodge the only objections to the destruction. Ghost hunters Docia Schultz Williams and Reneta Byrne write that wraiths from the "other side" lodged their own complaints as well: "Late one evening [before the Galera was] destroyed, guests at the Menger Hotel watched in shocked amazement as spectral forms marched, perhaps in protest of the desecration, along the walls of the rooms."[6]

In 1894, a newspaper article reported that the Alamo ghosts were acting up once again:

There is nothing new about the stories being told. There is the same measured tread of the ghostly sentry as he crosses the south side of the roof from east to west . . . the only variation appears to be in the fact that the sound of the feet on the roof had been heard as late as 5 o'clock in the morning by the officer in charge, who says that, as a matter of fact, however, the sounds are never heard except on rainy, drizzly nights.[7]

It must be interjected here that almost all of the security guards who have protected the grounds of the Alamo have told similar stories and have heard the same footsteps on the roof. Of course, even to the believer in ghosts, this story presents a problem: At the time of the battle, the Alamo had no roof. So the spectral sentry must date from a later time, and must have suffered from peculiar orders. The roof of the church has always been peaked or sloped—neither very conducive to sentry marching. Of course, I suppose if we accept that a ghost is on constant sentry duty at the Alamo, it doesn't stretch credulity much more to believe that he can do it wherever he wants.

The same *San Antonio Express* article described a visit to the Alamo by one Leon Mareschal and his 14-year-old daughter Mary, who was a psychic. At the time, the Alamo was being used as a jail and an informal police headquarters. The Mareschals presented themselves to Police Captain Jacob Coy, told him they knew that the Alamo was haunted, and offered to clear the spirits out of the place. Captain Coy, a clear-thinking man, believed that what the Alamo needed was fewer and better ghosts; so he told the helpful Mareschals to, by all means, do their stuff.

Little Mary went into a trance and soon announced, in so many words, that she saw dead people. Captain Coy asked who they were. She replied, "The forms say that they are the spirits of the defenders of the Alamo." Coy asked, reasonably enough, what they wanted.

Mary, still in a trance, said, "They say that there is buried in the walls of the building $50,000 in $20 gold pieces. They also say that they are anxious to have the money discovered and have been waiting for a chance to communicate with the people on earth about it and have it discovered. They will relinquish all claim to the treasure in favor of the person who finds it."

Instead of asking Mary what ghosts would do with the money anyway, Captain Coy asked, possibly with a certain gleam in his eye, "Now just where is the money buried?"

Mary pointed toward a "dingy little apartment in the southwest corner of the Alamo" and said, "It's in the wall of that—" and, darn the luck, she abruptly awoke from her trance.

With that anticlimactic scene, the matter of Alamo treasure seemed to be closed until a century later, when treasure hunter Frank T. Buschbacher went digging for gold and/or silver and/or sewage pipes in Alamo Plaza in 1993. He found nothing, apparently because he ignored the very explicit directions given by little Mary Mareschal in 1894.

Three years later, if Alamo ghosts didn't still walk the grounds, at least Alamo ghost stories were still being told with gusto. A lighthearted 1897 newspaper article tells of a tourist group that gets the full tour—including tales of history, heroes, and h'ants:

> As a climax to their visit the tourists are told the story of the ghosts of the Alamo and are shown the dark, gloomy recesses in the rear of the building where moans and hissing whispers and the clanking of chains are sometimes heard on wild stormy nights. The disturbing specters are supposed to be those of the errant monks who cried in chains for violating their monastic holiness in the old days when the Alamo was a Franciscan mission. That ghosts haunt the Alamo is claimed to be a well substantiated fact . . . some time ago, a number of prominent spiritualists held an all night séance there and are said to have had a very interesting and profitable conversation with the specters.[8]

Unfortunately for the supernatural-minded, "prominent spiritualists" are no longer welcome at the Alamo, at least not in a professional capacity. Several prominent parapsychologists—including Hans Holzer, arguably the most famous of them all—have applied to the DRT for permission to hold a séance within the Alamo. All have been refused.

It may be just as well. Most of the Alamo ghost stories that have seen print in recent years lack the *je ne sais quoi* of earlier tales. Now, instead of ghostly protesters marching around a building about to be razed, or diablos with burning swords, we have reports of John Wayne wandering about the place quoting dialogue from *The Alamo* (although, admittedly, it could be worse: Wayne's ghost could be spouting lines from *The Conqueror*).

In 1991, newspaper writer Craig Phelon accompanied local psychic Joe Holbrook to the Alamo to see if Wayne was indeed on the premises and, if so, just what he had to say for himself. Interestingly, though Holbrook didn't spot John Wayne, he did find six dead Mexican soldiers lounging about in the room to the left of the entrance. Three of these soldiers of Santa Anna gave Holbrook their names, which for the record were brothers Pablo and Raoul Fuentes and their pal Pedro Escobar. The other three apparently had better things to do and continued to wander in and out of the room, chatting of this and that. Holbrook asked the three cooperative soldiers if they knew Duke Wayne, and—it's a small afterlife—it turns out they did.

One of the ex-soldiers mentioned that Wayne likes the Alamo because "it rejuvenates him in some way. To him, the Alamo stands for the freedom of all mankind. He considers this the guts of freedom right here. That's his phrase."[9]

The ex-soldiers also pointed out that Duke wasn't around on this particular day; it seems that even spooks need a little down time. But they were able to fill the psychic in on what Wayne had been up to. Interestingly, the way they told it, he spends a lot of time chatting with Santa Anna—who, as it turns out, is pretty misunderstood. "In fact, Wayne says that he would have made the movie very differently if he knew then about the battle what he knows now."[10] Who knows what this means exactly, but I interpret it to indicate that Santa Anna has been urging Wayne to ditch James Edward Grant.

In addition to the information just described, the ghosts gave Holbrook some exciting news: "all the spirits connected with the Battle of the Alamo are planning to convene there for a sort of spirit reunion in 2002."[11]

So mark your calendars. Be there or be square.

The Alamo to Come

hen most visitors come to the Alamo, they are there to celebrate its rich history—though the history they're usually celebrating has to do with that famous fracas of 1836. The truth is, the
Alamo has never really been out of the action. Over the past century or
more, it has continually attracted bloodshed, violence, vandalism, and
silliness. It has served as a solemn backdrop for virtually every social
and political voice in Texas. The Alamo's ancient face has looked upon
class reunions and Ku Klux Klan rallies, presidential speeches and antiwar protests. Its doors have been set aflame by vandals—indeed, *people*
have been set aflame there—and its monuments urinated on by rock
stars. The Alamo became famous for its battle, but lesser battles are still
fought there all the time. Even when things aren't getting violent at the
Alamo, it remains a place of importance and power, a virtual blank slate
onto which anyone can write the social or political message of their
choice. The Alamo is not only a window to the past; it is a finger pointing toward the future.

The Alamo has always been a political place, of course. The battle in
1836 has remained a flashpoint of ethnic bitterness. Sometimes, perhaps
combined with liquor and tough talk, that bitterness still raises its ugly
head. In 1996, a drunken dispute over Texas history ended in gunfire
and death. Kevin Lee Newton, 33, and Richard Roland Ruiz, 35, were
"drinking buddies," but after drinking all day, they began to fight.
Things escalated until Newton went home, followed by Ruiz. While
Ruiz stood in Newton's yard, challenging him to come out, Newton got
his gun, stepped outside, and shot Ruiz point blank. Ruiz was armed
only with a can of beer. Sheriff's Department Captain Kenneth Billhartz

explained the origins of the murder: "They got into an argument," he said, "about whether the Anglos had stolen Texas from Mexico and what happened at the battle of the Alamo."[1]

There have certainly been many such arguments over the decades, and there will undoubtedly be many more. Happily, they don't often end in murder. But the fact remains that while many Texans remember the Alamo with sentiment and pride, to other Texans it is a symbol of bitterness and division. Perceived negative portrayals of the Tejano Alamo defenders in the IMAX production *Alamo . . . the Price of Freedom* (1988) led to demonstrations at the Alamo IMAX Theater and boycotts of the film's sponsors, Luby's Cafeterias Inc. and Pace Foods. One protestor stood outside the theater on opening day and borrowed a bit of traditional Alamo imagery from William Barret Travis: "All of you who will join in our boycott of Luby's, cross this line!"

The reaction to the film inspired considerable debate over the following months, not only about how Hispanic characters have been depicted in the history books, but how they have been characterized in the myth of the Alamo simply as villains, an "overwhelming gothic enemy."

The debate transcended the merely theoretical in 1989, when the League of United Latin American Citizens (LULAC) proposed that the Alamo be taken out of the hands of the DRT and given over to LULAC. Jose Garcia de Lara, Texas president of LULAC, said:

> the traditional attitude of the Alamo needs to be changed by research, revising the history books so our children may grow up with pride that we were a part of the fight for freedom. There have been very strong feelings against Hispanics because of the way the Alamo was portrayed. The [IMAX] movie, I guess, was the straw that broke the camel's back.[2]

A few years later, in 1993, the DRT found itself under siege in the Alamo once again. Democratic Rep. Ron Wilson filed legislation that would take the Alamo away from the Daughters and turn it over to the Texas Parks and Wildlife Department, which already controls the other four San Antonio missions. However, the legislation was easily defeated, partly because most Texans hold the DRT in very high regard and partly because Parks and Wildlife, under severe budget constraints,

A proposed reconstruction of Alamo Plaza. This plan would rebuild most of the original Alamo compound and turn the present San Antonio Post Office into an historical museum. Courtesy of *San Antonio Express-News*.

had just proposed closing eleven parks and merging eighteen others.[3]

Politics at the Alamo, however, are not always so negative. The shrine has been an essential whistle-stop for virtually every president and presidential candidate of the twentieth century. President William McKinley gave a speech in front of the Alamo in 1901. He reportedly pronounced it "ah-LAY-mo" but he was probably forgiven, what with being a Yankee and all. In 1930, proud city officials took President Calvin Coolidge there. In an instance where it might have been better for "Silent Cal" to remain silent, Coolidge asked, "What was it built for?" John F. Kennedy visited there in 1956, giving rise to a priceless (and possibly apocryphal) anecdote. Standing inside the church, Kennedy sought to avoid the pressing crowd waiting out front. He asked if there wasn't a back door he could use. "Senator," he was told, "if the Alamo had a back door, there wouldn't have been so many heroes!"

The Alamo was the site of several antiwar protests during the Vietnam era; and in 1971, the Monoxide Mummers Mime Troupe gave an impromptu performance on the lawn in front of the church. They were protesting freeway construction. The mime troupe was dispersed when the Alamo staff turned on the sprinklers. "We just don't allow people to walk on the grass," a spokesman said. "We really do work hard to keep our grass pretty."[4] In 1983 the Ku Klux Klan, a group even sillier than the Monoxide Mummers—but substantially more sinister— sought to hold its own march at the Alamo to stop the Red Brigade from raising the red flag over the shrine. The Klan was allowed to march on May 1, surrounded by 500 police officers who kept them moving along a three-block route, and they weren't allowed near the Alamo. But when the Klan applied for a second permit, San Antonio mayor Henry Cisneros said, "I think we have fulfilled our obligation to allow them free speech. We're not going to put this city through that kind of trauma for a bunch of idiots."[5]

The Klan march is a repugnant event in Alamo history, but other events are even more bizarre. In 1988, a man leaped out of a taxi at Alámo Plaza with guns in each hand and started blazing away. San Antonio resident Marvin Duncan, 55, wounded four people before police shot him and took him into custody. A witness said, "All hell broke loose. He had two guns in his hands. I've never seen anything like that. The guy was acting like John Wayne."[6] A couple of years later, a similarly disturbed individual sought to do damage to the Alamo itself, first by calling in a bomb threat, then by pouring a flammable liquid on the sidewalk at the north end of the property. The unnamed suspect was seen driving a pickup truck in the wrong lane on Houston Street. He parked near the Emily Morgan Hotel and poured "a milky fluid" on the sidewalk from a white plastic bucket. When he saw a security guard approaching, he jumped back into his truck and sped away.[7] A suspect was arrested two days later, charged with criminal attempt to commit arson, and held on $50,000 bond.[8]

And then there was rock star Ozzy Osbourne, who poured a fluid of a much different sort on the ground near the Alamo. On the night of February 19, 1982, Osbourne was taking a post-concert stroll through the streets of San Antonio. Some claim that he was dressed in drag for the occasion—pink tights and ballerina slippers, to be precise—but his arresting officer always claimed that Ozzy was dressed in gender-suitable clothing. He had apparently consumed a Homeric amount of alcohol and was at a level of intoxication for which there is no accurate gauge. Feeling—as one might under the circumstances—the call of

nature, Ozzy stepped up to the nearest wall, unzipped, and was immediately relieved. He was then immediately arrested. Legend normally has
it that Osbourne peed on the Alamo, but this is not quite accurate. He
actually urinated on the Alamo cenotaph across the plaza, which is by
any standard a lesser offense. As part of his punishment, Ozzy
Osbourne was banned from performing in the Alamo City. The ban was
lifted a decade later, after he contributed $10,000 to the DRT. During
his 1992 concert at Freeman Coliseum, his behavior was apparently
beyond reproach.[9]

The Alamo has had its heroic past, but it has also witnessed the most
amazing tomfoolery and nonsense, sinister deeds, and repugnant gestures. As Texas's most powerful symbol, it will undoubtedly continue to
act as a lightning rod, attracting extraordinary occurrences and people.

But what does the future hold for the Alamo? It would be foolhardy
to predict anything with certainty, of course. But it seems likely that historical interpretation of the site will continue to improve. For all its
great work in taking care of the shrine, the DRT has often come under
justifiable criticism for neglecting new Alamo findings in favor of celebrating only the heroic legends. Over the past few years, especially since
the sesquicentennial in 1986, educational and interpretive displays have
been cropping up with satisfying regularity. The "Wall of History"
beside the museum/gift shop is an excellent overview of Alamo history
that extends long before and after the 1836 battle. The exhibits in the
Long Barracks Museum have also been steadily upgraded. Too many
visitors still walk away with only a vague idea of what happened there,
or what the original fort actually looked like; but improvements are
many, and welcome.

There has been at least one major effort to transform the entire
nature of the property by rebuilding the original mission compound to
give tourists a much clearer picture of what the Alamo should be. A
massive 1994 proposal would have pushed back the buildings across the
plaza to allow a reconstruction of the original west wall and south-wall
gate. And the current post office building would be turned into a comprehensive Alamo museum. Though the plans were impressive and tantalizing, the logistics were simply too daunting, and the idea was
dropped.

But that doesn't mean it will stay dropped. The Alamo could only
benefit from being made a bit more remote, more serene. It has always

been slightly disconcerting to visitors to find that it stands in the very busiest part of a busy modern city. Reconstructing the walls of the original mission compound would do more than help visitors interpret history. It would create a different, more peaceful, contemplative atmosphere—the perfect place not only to learn the facts about the Alamo but also to meditate on its meaning, inspirational or otherwise.

Of course, a debate on just what that meaning is will also be a part of the Alamo of the future. Little by little, the myth is expanding, allowing a celebration not only of the holy trinity of Crockett, Travis, and Bowie, but an appreciation for the Tejano defenders, the soldiers and officers of Santa Anna, the women and children of the fort, and the people of color. The Alamo is no longer an exclusive myth. As we learn more about what actually happened during those thirteen days, we find that it was a complex event enacted by people of all different kinds, different ages, different colors. Out of the horror and pain of the past can be born a new understanding and appreciation for all the people who had a part in the founding of Texas. By admitting all of those many participants and their diverging viewpoints into the myth, we don't dilute the legend of the Alamo; we just give ourselves more heroes.

Appendices

Appendix 1: A Select Alamo Bibliography

This is by no means a comprehensive bibliography of books related to the Alamo—such a list would require a pretty hefty volume of its own. But for the reader who wishes to get a broad overview of the subject, the following books make up a solid library of Alamo history, fiction, folklore, and popular culture.

Chemerka, William R. *Alamo Almanac & Book of Lists*. Austin, Texas: Eakin Press, 1997. (History and popular culture)

Cousins, Margaret. *We Were There at the Battle of the Alamo*. New York: Grosset & Dunlap, 1958. (Juvenile fiction)

Davis, William C. *Three Roads to the Alamo*. New York: HarperCollins, 1998. (History)

Dobie, J. Frank, Mody C. Boatright, and Harry H. Ransom, eds. *In the Shadow of History*. Dallas: Texas Folklore Society, 1939. (History)

Edmondson, J. R. *The Alamo Story: From Early History to Recent Conflicts*. Plano, Texas: Republic of Texas Press, 2000. (History)

Frazee, Steve. *The Alamo*. New York: Avon Books, 1960. (Fiction)

Graham, Don. *Cowboys and Cadillacs: How Hollywood Looks at Texas*. Austin, Texas: TexasMonthly Press, 1983. (Popular culture)

Groneman, Bill. *Defense of a Legend: Crockett and the de la Pena Diary*. Plano, Texas: Republic of Texas Press, 1994. (History)

———. *Eyewitness to the Alamo*. Plano, Texas: Republic of Texas Press, 1996. (History)

Hardin, Stephen L. *Texian Iliad*. Austin, Texas: University of Texas Press, 1996. (History)

Harrigan, Stephen. *The Gates of the Alamo.* New York: Alfred A. Knopf, 2000. (Fiction)

Huffines, Alan C. *Blood of Noble Men: The Alamo Siege and Battle—An Illustrated Chronology.* Illustrated by Gary S. Zaboly. Austin, Texas: Eakin Press, 1999. (History)

Kilgore, Dan. *How Did Davy Die?* College Station, Texas: Texas A&M Press, 1978. (History)

Lehrer, James. *Viva Max.* New York: Duell, Sloan and Pearce, 1966. (Fiction)

Long, Jeff. *Duel of Eagles.* New York: William Morrow, 1990. (History)

Lord, Walter. *A Time to Stand.* New York: Harper & Brothers, 1961. (History)

Myers, John. *The Alamo.* New York: E. P. Dutton, 1948. (History)

De la Pena, Jose Enrique. *With Santa Anna in Texas: A Personal Narrative of the Revolution.* Translated and edited by Carmen Perry. Expanded edition, College Station, Texas: Texas A&M Press, 1997. (History)

Nelson, George. *The Alamo: An Illustrated History.* Dry Frio Canyon, Texas: Aldine Press, 1998. (History)

Schoelwer, Susan Prendergast, and Tom W. Glaser. *Alamo Images: Changing Perceptions of a Texas Experience.* Dallas: DeGolyer Library and Southern Methodist University Press, 1985. (History and popular culture)

Thompson, Frank. *Alamo Movies.* East Berlin, Pennsylvania: Old Mill Books, 1991. (Popular culture)

Tinkle, Lon. *Thirteen Days to Glory: The Siege of the Alamo.* New York: McGraw-Hill, 1958. (History)

Todish, Tim J. and Terry S. Todish. *Alamo Sourcebook 1836.* Austin, Texas: Eakin Press, 1998. (History)

Warren, Robert Penn. *Remember the Alamo!* New York: Random House, 1958. (Juvenile history)

Appendix 2: Alamo Films

This is a chronological list of films and television productions whose plots directly concern either the battle of the Alamo, or simply the Alamo itself. I have listed only those in which the Alamo is both featured and has an impact upon the story, and not those in which the Alamo simply appears as a backdrop; which is why *Pee-wee's Big Adventure* (1985) is included and *Selena* (1997) isn't. Neither have I listed Alamo documentaries, such as Arthur Drooker's superb *The Alamo* (1996) for the History Channel, or episodic TV productions (such as *The Time Tunnel,* from 1966). For more information on most of these films, please refer to my book *Alamo Movies* (1991, Old Mill Books;

2nd ed. 1994, Republic of Texas Press). Films marked with an asterisk (*) are available on video.

The Immortal Alamo (1911) One-reel film
The Siege and Fall of the Alamo (1914) Feature film
Martyrs of the Alamo (1915) Feature film
Tracy the Outlaw (1926) Feature film
Davy Crockett at the Fall of the Alamo (1926) Feature film
Heroes of the Alamo (1937) Feature film
The Alamo: Shrine of Texas Liberty (1938) Two-reel film
Man of Conquest (1939) Feature film
San Antonio (1945) Feature film
The Man From the Alamo (1953) Feature film
"You Are There: The Defense of the Alamo" (1953) Television production
Davy Crockett, King of the Wild Frontier (1955) Feature film, compiled from the television productions "Davy Crockett, Indian Fighter" (1954), "Davy Crockett Goes to Congress" (1955), and "Davy Crockett at the Alamo" (1955).
The Last Command (1955) Feature film
The Alamo (1960) Feature film
"Spirit of the Alamo" (1960) Television production
Viva Max (1966) Feature film
"You Are There: The Siege of the Alamo" (1971) Television production
The Spirit of Independence (1976) Cartoon
"Seguin" (1982) Television production
Cloak and Dagger (1984) Feature film
Pee-wee's Big Adventure (1985) Feature film
Gone to Texas, a.k.a. Houston: The Legend of Texas (1986) Television movie
The Alamo: 13 Days to Glory (1987) Television movie
Alamo . . . the Price of Freedom (1988) IMAX film
*"James A. Michener's Texas" (1994) Television mini-series
Two for Texas (1998) Television movie
*"Dear America: A Line in the Sand" (2000) Television production

Appendix 3: Selected Alamo Theatrical Works

Unknown. *The Fall of the Alamo or Texas and the Oppressors* (1836) Play
Acheson, Sam. *We Are Besieged* (1941) Play
Baber, Ralph K. *The Silenced Cannon* (1992) Outdoor drama
de Helen, Sandra. *My Alamo* (1999) One-act play
Linkletter, A. G. (book and lyrics) and Emil Gerstenberger (music). *America!*

Cavalcade of a Nation (1940). Pageant written for the Golden Gate International Exposition, San Francisco, California.

Martin, Franklin Y. *Death Comes to the Alamo: The Last Hour of Travis and his Immortals* (1935) Play

Mayer, Edwin Justus. *Sunrise in My Pocket, or, The Last Days of Davy Crockett* (1941) Play

Mayes, May Abney and Willie Megee McGhee (libretto); Theosophus Fitz (music). *Tejas: A Dramatic Opera in Three Acts Commemorating the 100th Anniversary of Texas* (1936) Opera

McLane, Hiram H. *The Capture of the Alamo: A Historical Tragedy, in Four Acts, with Prologue* (1886) A play in verse

Nona, Francis. *The Fall of the Alamo, An Historical Drama in Four Acts* (1879) Play

Strickler, Jerry. *My Alamo Family* (1986) One-man play

Taylor, Bernard J. (words and music). *Liberty! The Siege of the Alamo* (1999) Musical play

Warren, Steve. *Gone to Texas* (1986). The Crockett monologue in this production was expanded in 1995 for the play *Me, Davy Crockett*.

Yelvington, Ramsey. *A Cloud of Witnesses* [also known as *The Drama of the Alamo*] (1954) Play

Appendix 4: Selected Alamo Poems

The Alamo has had extraordinarily bad luck when it comes to poetry. With a few exceptions, most of the following are barely tolerable—mawkish, cloying, and far from subtle. However, as in most elements of the popular-culture aspect of the Alamo, quality is of lesser consideration than content. Some of the poems were written in the wake of the Alamo battle, and they give us an invaluable voice from the culture that lived through the period and responded to the event. Others have played free with the Alamo myth and highlighted interesting, if sometimes heavy-handed, new facets of the cultural experience. A few of the poems here are truly great, like Michael Lind's *The Alamo: An Epic*. A few, like Morton Watts Simms's *The Maid of the Alamo, or, The Incarnation of Chivalry,* are so silly that they are little treasures in themselves (the amateurish, school-pageant-level photographs in this 1913 volume make it priceless to devotees of Alamo kitsch). The bottom line is, when it comes to poetry about the Alamo, caveat emptor.

Anonymous. *A New "Welcome to the Bower"* (1837)
Anonymous. *San Antonio (Written in the Ruins of the Alamo)* (1840)

Anonymous. *Texians, To Your Banner Fly* (1836)
Anonymous. *To Santa Anna* (1836)
Anonymous. *War Song* (1836)
Berry, Viola R. *The Alamo* (1906)
Bowman, Jonathan. *The Alamo: The Cradle of Texas Liberty* (1897)
Brogan, Evelyn. *James Bowie: A Hero of the Alamo* (1922)
Cosby, Amy Pearl. *Crockett in the Alamo* (ca. 1909)
Farr, Alvan E. *The Alamo* (ca. 1909)
Forbes, G. V. H. *The Texian War Cry* (1836)
Gray, Edward McQueen. *Alamo* (1898)
Heavenhill, William S. *Siege of the Alamo: A Mexico-Texan Tale* (1888)
Hyer, Julien C. *The Alamo—1836* (1941)
Lind, Michael. *The Alamo: An Epic Poem* (1998)
Parmenter, Stephen C. *Texian Hymn of Liberty* (1838)
Porter, Jenny L. *Siege of the Alamo* (1981)
Potter, Reuben M. *Hymn of the Alamo* (1836)
Rice, Grantland. *Ghosts of the Alamo* (ca. 1917)
Roche, James Jeffrey. *The Men of the Alamo* (ca. 1917)
Watts, Morton Simms. *The Maid of the Alamo or, The Incarnation of Chivalry* (1913)

Appendix 5: Selected Alamo Songs and Recordings

When it comes to Alamo music, silliness and sentiment often go hand in hand. Listening to some of these musical pieces can be giddily entertaining if you're in the proper frame of mind, and sometimes appalling if you're not. A few of them are genuinely good. No matter what you may think of John Wayne's *The Alamo,* the score by Dimitri Tiomkin is a magnificent work; so is Don Gillis's long-neglected 1947 symphonic piece *The Alamo.* On a slightly less exalted plane, no baby boomer can remain unmoved by "The Ballad of Davy Crockett"; and it's also hard to resist Jane Bowers's "Remember the Alamo," with its memorable lyrics: "Hi-yup! Santy Anny, we're killin' your soldiers below, so men wherever they go, will remember the Alamo!" Most of the following recordings are out of print, but the industrious antique hunter can still round up many of them. Some of the earlier sheet music is harder to come by, and a lot of it is quite valuable—for reasons that usually don't have much to do with the quality of the songs.

"The Alamo" (1895) Patriotic song and chorus. Words by Mrs. Jennie Myers. Music by Miss Ella Rodeffer.

The Alamo (1947). Symphonic work composed by Don Gillis. LP

The Alamo (1960). Motion picture score composed by Dimitri Tiomkin. LP and CD reissue.

"The Alamo" (1964) Spoken word/song. Lorne Greene, from "Welcome to the Ponderosa." LP

"The Alamo" (1986). Song. Words and music by Eric von Schmidt.

Alamo . . . the Price of Freedom (1988). Motion picture score composed by Merrill Jensen. Audiocassette and CD

"Alamo Rag" (1910) Song. Lyrics by Ben Deely; music by Percy Wenrich. Edison cylinder recording and 78-rpm recording

"Alamo Serenade" (1938) Song. Words and music by Eileen Pike.

"The Ballad of the Alamo" (1960) Song. Music by Dimitri Tiomkin; lyrics by Paul Francis Webster. Recorded by Frankie Avalon, Stanley Black, Marty Robbins, The Sons of Texas, The Easy Riders, and others.

"The Ballad of Davy Crockett" (1954). Song. Lyrics by Tom Blackburn; music by George Bruns. Recorded by Bill Hayes, Fess Parker, Tennessee Ernie Ford, Tex Ritter, Burl Ives, Patti Page, the Sons of the Pioneers, and over thirty other artists.

Davy Crockett. Dramatized story on LP. Felicity Trotman & Shirley Greenway

Davy Crockett at the Alamo (1955). Dramatized story based on Walt Disney's "Disneyland" episode of the same title. Featuring the voices of Fess Parker and Buddy Ebsen. Released on 78-rpm recording and on LP.

The Last Command (1955). Motion picture score composed by Max Steiner. LP

The Legend of Davy Crockett (1977). Dramatized story. The Tarrytowne Players. LP

"Remember the Alamo" (1908). Song. Words and music by Jessie Beattie Thomas.

"Remember the Alamo" (1957). Song by Jane Bowers. Recorded by Johnny Cash, Donovan, The Kingston Trio, Willie Nelson, Tex Ritter, and many others.

"Remember the Alamo" (1960). Song by Rich Gehr and Terry Gilkyson. Recorded by The Easy Riders on their LP of the same name. This recording also includes several songs from John Wayne's film, *The Alamo* (1960). LP

Remember the Alamo (1960). Dramatized story narrated by Claude Rains. Script by Michael Avallone; music by Tony Mottola. LP.

Remember the Alamo (1967). Dramatized story. True Action Adventure Series, produced by Sonny Lester. LP

"Somewhere in Mexico (Remember the Alamo)" (1916). Song. Words and music by Francis J. Lowe.

The Stories of the Pioneers. Dramatized story. The T.V. Theater Players. LP

"Stout and High" (1988). The Wagoneers, LP and CD. Song "Stout and High" by Monte Warden.

Viva Max (1968). Motion picture score composed by Hugo Montenegro. LP

Western Playhouse: Songs and Stories of the Great Wild West (no date given)
   Dramatic stories and songs. Stories adapted by Roberta Strauss; music by
   Bill Simon and his Frontiersmen. Includes songs and stories about several
   Western heroes, including Jim Bowie and Davy Crockett. LP

Notes

Introduction

1. Susan Prendergast Schoelwer and Tom W. Glaser, eds. *Alamo Images: Changing Perceptions of a Texas Experience* (Dallas: DeGolyer Library and Southern Methodist University Press, 1985), p. 3.

2. Stephen L. Hardin. Texian Iliad (Austin, Texas: University of Texas Press, 1994), p. 131.

3. There are several variations on the spelling of Dickinson's name. For simplicity's sake, I have chosen this one and will use it throughout the book, although it is spelled differently in many of the plays, poems, books, and films discussed.

4. I recommend the interested reader go to Stephen L. Hardin's excellent examination of, and attack on, the Nuñez account in *Southwestern Historical Quarterly*, July 1990.

5. *San Antonio Daily Express* (30 June 1889).

6. *San Antonio Daily Express* (12 May 1907).

7. Clara Driscoll. *In the Shadow of the Alamo* (New York: The Knickerbocker Press, 1906), pp. 33, 38, 41.

8. Ibid., p. 47.

9. Maurice Elfer. *The Heroic Story of the Alamo* (Chicago: Schwartkopf Mimeo Service, 1938), pp 10–11.

10. William Zinsser. *American Places* (New York: HarperCollins, 1992), p. 67.

11. William H. McNeill, "Mythistory, or Truth, Myth, History, and Historians," *American Historical Review* 91 (February 1986): 7.

Chapter One: The Mission

1. Adina de Zavala. *History and Legends of the Alamo and Other Missions in and around San Antonio* (Houston: Arte Publico Press, 1996), p. 4.

2. Ibid., p. 6.

3. George Nelson. *The Alamo: An Illustrated History* (Dry Frio Canyon, Texas: Aldine Press, 1998), p. 6.

4. de Zavala, *History and Legends of the Alamo,* p. 7.

Chapter Two: The Fortress

1. Jack Jackson. *Los Tejanos* (Stamford, Connecticut.: Fantagraphic Books, Inc., 1982), p. 36.

2. Walter Lord. *A Time to Stand* (New York: Harper & Brothers, 1961), p. 85.

3. Ibid., pp. 200–201.

4. Ibid.

5. The Alamo garrison was loaded with former lawyers. In retrospect, it might have been a better idea for them to sue Santa Anna than fight him; they certainly would have had the manpower to do *that.*

6. Lord, *A Time to Stand,* pp. 112–113 (photo caption).

7. Thomas Ricks Lindley, "James Butler Bonham," *Alamo Journal*, no. 62, August 1988.

8. Lord, *A Time to Stand,* p. 203.

9. R. R. Blake, "A Vindication of Rose and His Story," in J. Frank Dobie, *In the Shadow of History* (Austin: Texas Folklore Society, 1939; fascimile ed. 1980), p. 34.

10. Lord, *A Time to Stand,* p. 204.

11. For complete transcriptions of all the survivors' testimonies, let me recommend two excellent books: *The Blood of Noble Men*, by

Alan Huffines with wonderful illustrations by Gary Zaboly; and *Eyewitness to the Alamo,* by Bill Groneman. See the bibliography for full information.

12. This is not the place to detail the debate over the de la Pena "diary." For a thorough look at the pros and cons, refer to Bill Groneman's *Defense of a Legend: Crockett and the de la Pena Diary* (which asserts that the document is probably a forgery) and James E. Crisp's introduction to the expanded edition of *With Santa Anna in Texas,* Carmen Perry's translation of de la Pena's work. Crisp believes that the "diary" is probably genuine. For full details, see the bibliography.

13. Paul Andrew Hutton, "Introduction" *Alamo Images: Changing Perceptions of a Texas Experience* (Dallas: DeGolyer Library and Southern Methodist University Press, 1985), p. 13.

Chapter Three: From Army Headquarters to Department Store

1. Letter to Capt. Comdt. S. M. Howe, San Antonio Béxar, 3 July 1847.

2. *San Antonio Express* (9 April 1905).

3. Quoted in Donald E. Everett, *San Antonio: the Flavor of Its Past, 1845–1898* (San Antonio: Trinity University Press, 1975), p. 18.

4. For some of this information on Everett, I am indebted to Kevin R. Young's biographical sketch in *The Handbook of Texas Online,* 1999.

5. George Nelson. *The Alamo: An Illustrated History* (Dry Frio Canyon, Texas: Aldine Press, 1998), p. 59.

6. Ibid.

7. Ibid.

8. Michael and David Russi are, in their own right, important figures in San Antonio history. They worked with John Fries on many important buildings, including the French Building and the First Presbyterian Church. In addition to his substantial career as a contractor and stone mason, David Russi was for many years the chief of San Antonio Fire Association Number 1 and also served as alderman from the Second Ward on the San Antonio City Council.

9. Craig R. Covner, "From the Renaissance to the Alamo? A Speculation on an American Icon" (Paper from the author's collection).

10. Ibid.

11. Kevin R. Young, "Major Babbitt and the Alamo 'Hump'," *Military Images* (July–August 1984).

12. Alexander Edwin Sweet, "The Alamo," from his column "Texas Siftings," September 9, 1882. Reprinted in Alex Sweet's *Texas: The Lighter Side of Lone Star History,* Virginia Eisenhour, ed. (Austin: University of Texas Press, 1986), p. 11.

13. Maurice Elfer. *The Heroic Story of the Alamo* (Chicago: Schwartzkopf Mimeo Service, 1938), p. 10.

Chapter Four: The Second Battle of the Alamo

1. Adina de Zavala. *History and Legends of the Alamo and other Missions in and around San Antonio* (San Antonio: By the author, 1917. New edition: Houston: Arte Publico Press, 1996), p. 51.

2. Letter in the de Zavala [Adina] papers, Center for American History, University of Texas at Austin.

3. *San Antonio Express* (29 April 1900).

4. Clara Driscoll. *In the Shadow of the Alamo* (New York: Knickerbocker Press, 1906), p. 44.

5. *San Antonio Express* (n.d. November 1905).

6. DRT Report, 1907, pp. 23–24.

7. Letter from Charles M. Reeves to Adina de Zavala, September 21, 1906. In the de Zavala Papers, University of Texas at Austin.

Chapter Five: The Alamo of Poet and Playwright

1. Philip Graham, ed. *Early Texas Verse* (Austin: The Steck Co., 1936), p. xiii.

2. William S. Heavenhill. *Siege of the Alamo: A Mexico-Texan Tale* (San Antonio: Schulz & Schott, Printers), 1888.

3. Ibid.

4. Jenny Lind Porter. *The Siege of the Alamo* (Los Angeles: Pepperdine University Press, 1981), p. xiii.

5. Michael Lind, "On Epic." In *The Alamo: An Epic* (Boston, New York: Houghton Mifflin Co., 1997), p. 285.

6. Ibid., p. 312.

7. Ibid.

8. Ralph M. Alderman, ed. *The Letters of James Kirke Paulding* (Madison: University of Wisconsin Press, 1962), p. 113.

9. Michael A. Lofaro, ed. *Davy Crockett: The Man, The Legend, The Legacy, 1786–1986* (Knoxville: University of Tennessee Press, 1985), p. 108.

10. Ibid.

11. Paul Andrew Hutton, "Frontier Hero Davy Crockett," *Wild West Magazine,* February 1999, p. 40.

12. Walter Lord. *A Time to Stand* (New

York: Harper & Brothers, 1961), p. 171.

13. Hiram H. McLane, preface to *The Capture of the Alamo: A Historical Tragedy* (San Antonio: San Antonio Printing Co.), 1886.

14. Franklin Y. Martin, foreword to *Death Comes to the Alamo* (Dallas: Tardy Publishing Company), 1935.

15. *San Antonio Express* (6 March 1936).

16. Paul Baker, introduction to *A Cloud of Witnesses* (Austin: University of Texas Press, 1959), p. 7.

17. Ibid., p. 9.

18. *My Alamo* synopsis, provided to author via e-mail by Sandra de Helen.

19. *San Antonio Express-News* (9 November 1999), p. 10F.

20. Ibid.

21. Ibid.

22. *San Antonio Express-News* (11 November 1999).

23. George Duthie, play review of *The Scotsman* (undated).

Chapter Six: The Cinematic Alamo

1. Paul G. Levine, "Remember the Alamo?" *American Film,* January–February 1982, pp. 47–49.

2. *Los Angeles Times* (19 December 1987).

3. Ibid.

4. I am indebted to Brian Huberman for this interpretation.

5. *Film Index,* 26 February 1910, p. 3.

6. *Nickelodeon,* vol. V, no. 4, p. 114.

7. *Film Index,* 22 April 1911.

8. *Film Index,* 6 May 1911.

9. *New York Dramatic Mirror,* 19 July 1911.

10. *Film Index,* 15 April 1911.

11. *San Antonio Light,* 2 June 1914.

Chapter Seven: Fun and Games: Alamo Toys, Songs, and Souvenirs

1. *San Antonio Express and News* (29 April 1961).

2. Ibid.

Chapter Eight: Rebuilding the Alamo

1. *Houston Post* (27 March 1938).

2. *San Antonio Express* (18 February 1936).

3. Ibid.

4. *San Antonio Express* (21 February 1936).

5. Ibid.

6. *Dallas News* (17 October 1909), p. 28.

7. Ibid.

8. Ibid.

9. *Galveston News* (17 October 1909).

10. *San Antonio Express-News* (13 December 1987).

11. *San Antonio Express-News* (6 March 1999).

12. *San Antonio News* (8 March 1956).

13. Brian Huberman and Ed Hugetz, "Fabled Façade," *Southwest Media Review* (Spring 1985), p. 39.

Chapter Nine: Alamo Ghosts

1. *San Antonio Express* (9 April 1905).

2. William Brooker. *Texas: An Epitome of Texas History . . .* (Columbus, Ohio: Nitschke Bros., 1897).

3. Adina de Zavala. *History and Legends of the Alamo and other Missions in and around San Antonio* (San Antonio: By the author, 1917). Houston: Arte Publico Press, 1996 (new edition), p. 51.

4. Ibid., p. 52.

5. Ibid., p. 52.

6. Docia Schultz Williams and Reneta Byrne. *Spirits of San Antonio and South Texas* (Plano, Texas: Republic of Texas Press, 1993), p. 5.

7. *San Antonio Express* (5 February 1894).

8. *San Antonio Express* (23 August 1897).

9. Craig Phelon, "Are the Spirits of John Wayne and a host of other ghosts haunting the Alamo?" *San Antonio Express-News* (27 January 1991).

10. Ibid.

11. Ibid.

Chapter Ten: The Alamo to Come

1. *San Antonio Express-News* (2 August 1996).

2. Julie Catalano, "The Second Battle of the Alamo," *Vista,* 1989, p. 12.

3. *Austin American-Statesman* (2 March 1993).

4. *San Antonio Light* (7 February 1971).

5. *San Antonio Light* (14 May 1983).

6. *Vancouver Sun* (3 March 1988), p. A5.

7. *San Antonio Express-News* (30 April 1990).

8. *San Antonio Express-News* (1 May 1990).

9. *San Antonio Express-News* (4 September 1992).

Acknowledgments

The first time I visited the Alamo it was love at first sight. It was June 1963. My family and I had been traveling by car for two days from South Carolina and were welcomed to the outskirts of San Antonio by a blinding Texas thunderstorm. The rain came down in curtains so opaque and powerful that we had to pull over to the side of the road twice to wait until visibility returned.

Even under the circumstances, we had no problem finding the Alamo. Huge signs with arrows kept us on track—and my heart pounded with the idea that we were really there, that I would finally stand on the sacred ground I had dreamt of for so long. As we turned right from Commerce Street onto Alamo Street, the rain suddenly stopped. Within seconds, a brilliant late afternoon sun broke through the clouds. We pulled up to the curb in front of the ancient limestone church; and as I sprang from the car, the sunlight glanced off the wet walls and sidewalk puddles, creating a light show of electric rainbow colors so vivid that I had to take a second to allow my eyes to become used to it. The Alamo was alive with light, shimmering and golden.

If I was interested in the Alamo before that, I was fascinated from that moment on. Over the years, to my surprise, I discovered that others shared my obsession with the place—we all thought we were the only ones. As filmmaker David Zucker once said to me, referring to a scene in *Close Encounters of the Third Kind,* "We were all building our little mashed potato Alamos."

But once we Alamo fanatics found each other, many lasting relationships were formed. I have had hundreds, maybe thousands of discussions about the Alamo over my lifetime. Every one of them contributed in some way to my understanding of and appreciation for the Alamo of the past and present. Although I would like to acknowledge each of those friends, I don't have the space; and it would make mighty dull reading besides. But these folks listed here have given me so much, and I want to thank them all.

Paul Andrew Hutton is not only one of the great authorities on the historical Alamo, he's also a hearty enthusiast of the Alamo of pop culture. Naturally, we've seen eye to eye on most Alamo issues since we first met in 1987. Paul has more than once opened his collection, and his home, to me. He has consistently treated my constant barrage of questions and requests with patience, good humor, and boundless generosity. He has also been a great pal of mine and, although I try never to say anything to his face that isn't a veiled insult, behind his back I have to admit that I think the world of him and appreciate his friendship more than I can say.

Craig Covner and Nina Rosenstand also became my close friends through our mutual interest in the Alamo. They both possess an astonishingly broad knowledge of the subject, and our discussions have been so numerous and wide-ranging over the years that I should really give them co-author status. Except that would involve sharing my royalties, which I'm unwilling to do. Craig knows more about the physical Alamo than any other human on Earth, and I join many of his friends in urging him to write his own book one of these days. In the meantime, his help to me has been immense and his friendship even immenser, if that's a word. He is also, like me, a toy enthusiast, and is the first one I call when I've made some particularly terrific flea market—or eBay—acquisition.

Nearly every photograph in this book is here thanks to Marc Wanamaker of Bison Archives. Marc has been a generous and helpful friend on this, as he has on nearly all of my books. While relatively few photographs printed here actually came from Bison Archives, Marc produced dozens of prints and slides for me and otherwise made sure that every image was as top-notch as possible. Thanks for everything, Marc.

One of the great strongholds of Alamo knowledge and enthusiasm is in New Jersey, of all places, and I have to particularly thank some of my good friends there. William R. Chemerka has published the *Alamo Journal* for a decade and a half and has provided an invaluable clearinghouse of information about the Alamo. On a more personal level, he has been incredibly helpful to me and I value his friendship very much. Thanks, Colonel!

Mike and Nancy Boldt were there for me a decade ago when I was working on *Alamo Movies,* and we've remained pals ever since. They've put me up several times in their wonderful grand old house and have extended every form of hospitality and assistance. Mike and I have even collaborated on a couple of Alamo video projects—he's a fine musician and artist—and there are plenty more collaborations to come. Thanks to both of you.

And finally, Murray Weissmann, curator of the largest, most astonishing private archive related to the Alamo and Davy Crockett, has also been a great friend for a long time. I go to his house in much the same spirit as a Catholic goes to the Vatican, except that Murray almost never makes me kiss his ring. He's a knowledgeable, generous, and very acquisitive man. More important, he's a great guy and I like him very much.

And now for the Texans. Kevin R. Young, Steve Hardin, and Steve Harrigan have been friends of mine for well over a decade. They have all helped me in countless ways that range from priceless information to much-needed criticism to the use of a spare bedroom. And, of course, they have all produced works on the Alamo that are far greater than my own modest efforts, yet have always been kind enough to treat me as a peer as well as a pal.

The wonderful Joan Headley has been a warm and generous friend—and an indefatigable Alamo enthusiast. I've sent Joan packing all over the place getting photographs and other information for me, and she has shared priceless items from her own stunning collection, as well. I'm more grateful than I can say. Besides which, she's the only person I know who owns more dogs than I do.

My deepest love and gratitude go to my mother, Geraldine Thompson, and to my late father, Theodore Thompson. Thank you for introducing me to the Alamo in the first place, for taking me there as a child, and for encouraging my interest in the subject from the time I was yea high.

In addition, I must thank the following great people: Leith Adams; Bob Birchard; Dorothy Black; Kevin Brownlow; Quince Buteau; Wallace Chariton; Gina Chepely of International Center for Entrepreneurial Development; Donna and Mike Durrett; J. R. Edmondson; Jason Ehrlich; Michael Emmerich; John Andrew Gallagher; Sam Gill; Mary Elizabeth Sue Goldman; Bill Groneman; Hank Harrison; Sandra de Helen; Thomas W. Holland; Brian Huberman; Alan Huffines; Eric Jamborsky; Ronnie James; Jack Judson; Ken Mahoney; Tony Malanowski; Phil Martin; Joe Musso; Javier Nava, owner of the Alamo Ballroom & Convention Center, Inc.; Mary Norrod; Sheryl O'Connell; Fess Parker; Tony Pasqua; David Pierce; Ken Pruitt; Paul Reubens; Kay Scheer; the late, and very great, Happy Shahan; Gerald Shough; Michael Singer; Judith Sobre; Brian Taves; Bernard J. Taylor; John C. Tibbetts; Terry Todish; Tim Todish; Ashley Ward; Robert Weill; Gary Zaboly; William Zinsser; David Zucker; and Michael T. Zunno.

I also want to thank the staffs of the Ransom Center for the Humanities and the Barker Center for Western Studies, UT-Austin; the staff of the DRT Library at the Alamo, particularly Martha Utterback and the late Bernice Strong; the Institute of Texan Cultures; the Margaret Herrick Library of the Academy of Motion Picture Arts and Sciences; and the Library of Congress.

Of course, I especially want to thank my miracle of a wife, Claire, who makes life perfect in every way. And I want to urge Pete, Molly, and Jake never to surrender or retreat.

FRANK THOMPSON

Index

Frank Thompson

Frank Thompson is an author, comedy writer, filmmaker, and film historian. His books include *Abraham Lincoln: 20th Century Popular Portrayals* (Taylor Publishing, 1999), *The Great Christmas Movies* (Taylor, 1998), *I Was That Masked Man* (Taylor; 1996, co-author Clayton Moore), *Lost Films* (Citadel, 1996), *The Star Film Ranch: Texas' First Picture Show* (Republic of Texas Press, 1996), *Los Angeles Uncovered* (Seaside Press, 1996), *Henry King* (Directors Guild of America, 1995), *Robert Wise: A Bio-Bibliography* (1995), *Gregory La Cava* (Filmoteca Espanol, 1995; co-author), *Alamo Movies* (Republic of Texas Press, 1994), *Tim Burton's "The Nightmare Before Christmas"* (Hyperion, 1993), *Between Action And Cut: Five American Directors* (Scarecrow Press, 1985), and *William A. Wellman* (Scarecrow, 1983).

Thompson wrote and directed "The Great Christmas Movies" (1998) for American Movie Classics. He served as associate producer and historical consultant, and appears onscreen in "Wild Bill: Hollywood Maverick," an award-winning documentary about the career of William A. Wellman (1996, Turner Network Television). He also appears onscreen in E! Entertainment's "Louise Brooks" episode of *Mysteries and Scandals* (November 9, 1998), the History Channel documentary "The Alamo" (1996), and other cinema-related documentaries.

Thompson is currently a writer on the hit television series "Blind Date" (Universal Television). Other series television scripts include "Fast Food Films" (FX, 1999), "Reel Wild Cinema" (USA Network, 1996–1997), and "Hollywood Babylon" (syndicated, 1992). Thompson has written many introductory scripts for American Movie Classics and Romance Classics hosts such as Cher, Sharon Stone, Jodie Foster, Winona Ryder, Billy Bob Thornton, Martin Scorsese, Roddy McDowall, Kim Hunter, Stephanie Powers, Morgan Fairchild, Phyllis Diller, Brendan Fraser, Shirley Jones, Ali MacGraw, Kirsten Dunst, Lesley-Anne Down, Patrick Wayne, Lesley Ann Warren, Sean Young, and others. He wrote and co-produced *Frank Capra: A Personal Remembrance* (VidAmerica, 1992), and *The Making of "It's a Wonderful Life"* (Republic Pictures, 1991), both of which appear on the 1996 Republic Pictures Home Video release, *It's a Wonderful Life 50th Anniversary Edition.*

Thompson has contributed to several film encyclopedias and is a regular writer for magazines such as *American Cinematographer, American Film, Film Comment, Hollywood Reporter, Disney Channel Magazine, Sight and Sound, Tower Pulse!* and *Texas Monthly.* He has also written for many newspapers, notably *Atlanta Journal & Constitution, Miami Herald, Philadelphia Inquirer, San Francisco Chronicle, Boston Globe,* and *San Antonio Express News.*

Frank Thompson lives in Burbank, California, with his wife Claire and a virtual herd of pets.